LEWIS HINE

+ IN EUROPE +

THE LOST PHOTOGRAPHS

LEWIS HINE
✛ IN EUROPE ✛
THE "LOST" PHOTOGRAPHS

DAILE KAPLAN

ABBEVILLE PRESS PUBLISHERS
NEW YORK

Editor: Walton Rawls
Designer: Stephanie Bart-Horvath
Production Manager: Dana Cole

Library of Congress Cataloging-in-Publication Data:

Kaplan, Daile.
    Lewis Hine in Europe: the lost photographs / Daile Kaplan.
        p.   cm.
    Bibliography: p.
    Includes index.
    ISBN 0-89659-745-8
    1. Photography, Documentary—Europe.   2. Hine, Lewis
Wickes, 1874–1940.   I. Hine, Lewis Wickes, 1874–1940.
II. Title.
TR820.5.K36 1988
779'.092'4—dc19   88-959
                                                    CIP

A B B R E V I A T I O N S

AAA   Archives of American Art,
               Elizabeth McCausland Papers
               New York, N.Y.

ARC   American Red Cross
               National Headquarters
               Washington, D.C.

CAH   Commission on Archives and History
               The United Methodist Church
               Madison, N.J.

Folks Papers   Homer Folks Papers
               Butler Library, Columbia University
               New York, N.Y.

GEH   International Museum of Photography
               at George Eastman House
               Rochester, N.Y.

LC   Prints and Photographs Division
               American Red Cross Collection
               Library of Congress
               Washington, D.C.

Library   Manuscript Division
               Papers of the National
               Child Labor Committee
               Library of Congress
               Washington, D.C.

NYPL   The New York Public Library
               New York, N.Y.

SWHA   Social Welfare History Archives
               University of Minnesota
               Minneapolis, Minnesota

This book is dedicated to
my mother and father,
Irma and Edward Kaplan

C O N T E N T S

CONTENTS

Newsboy, New York City, 1910.
(Hine's shadow at bottom left)

Within the past twenty years, Lewis Wickes Hine has assumed his rightful position as one of America's principal twentieth-century photographers. He is best known for his moving photos of immigrant families on Ellis Island and New York's Lower East Side, of child laborers toiling in factories, farms, and mines throughout the United States, and of heroic workers balanced on girders of the Empire State Building. However, the purposes of this book are to place Hine's early work, photographs made between 1904 and 1919, within a broader historical context by charting his adoption of the "photo story" (his own term), and to reintroduce a "lost" cache of Hine's mature photographs, made in Europe during and after World War I, which I "discovered" in the Library of Congress.

Few historians have addressed the phenomenon of photojournalism in the United States, particularly in its initial manifestations in the late-nineteenth and early-twentieth centuries. Nor has there been adequate research and interpretative work on the implications of the photo story as a new language, one that joins photo and text. However, the development of the photo story is clearly reflected in Hine's development as a photojournalist.

From the inception of his career as a free-lance photographer for the National Child Labor Committee in 1906, to his editorial work for the Progressive journal *The Survey* in 1908, to his assignment as staff photographer for the American Red Cross in Europe in 1918 and 1919, Hine set out to make photographs for the printed page. By its focus on the "common" individual, its gathering of personal and descriptive information, and its assembling of the elements of photograph and caption into human-interest stories, Hine's work may be placed within an American tradition that is both humanistic and democratic.

Today we accept the vernacular orientation of Hine's work as photographic art. But, when Hine began working, the appearance of photography in Progressive and "quality" journals was limited. There were several reasons for this, not least of which was the general view at the turn of the century that photographs were unappealing documents that undermined propriety and good taste. In addition, economic and technical factors made the transmutation of photographs into printed halftones a costly process. Nevertheless, with the proliferation of popular illustrated magazines photographs began to appear with greater frequency. The use of photographs was, however, restricted in prestigious, "gentlemen's" journals since editors preferred the high "artistic" quality of drawings and etchings. In a sense, the reluctance to use social photographs in these journals may also be attributed to the public's inability to "read" them: photos were essentially seen as illustrations and dependent on the articles or text they embellished.

Although Hine was confident of the importance of "Hineography," he was not fully aware of his pioneering contributions as a photojournalist. While conflict, for example, permeates his pictures through 1919, he later referred to it as "my share of negative documentation." Yet, by locating photography within an American cultural tradition that was inextricably linked to journalism, he was the first photographer to "picture" the common man, woman, and child in a positive light, and to incorporate their point of view, their "voice," in his captions. In addition, he was responsible for developing a modern vernacular aesthetic (street photography) and a form (the human-interest photo story) that gave rise to photography as a new tool.

From the beginning, Hine's work empowered his subjects and defused negative associations about photography. Later on, with the appearance of his photo stories, Hine disassembled the social photograph into syntactical units of picture and text, and reorganized it into a viable communications form. He produced substantive, controversial images that, nonetheless, evoked qualities easily identifiable and shared: dignity, grace, and beauty. By arranging a group of images in multipage graphic designs, he recognized the latent power of the iconological image (along with authoritative text) as an effective and compelling graphic language.

An examination of the pictures that Hine produced between 1904 and 1919 exposes three widespread misconceptions about photojournalism: first, that it was made possible by the manufacture of small, hand-held 35mm cameras; second, that it first appeared in the United States with the publications of *Life* and *Look* magazines in the 1930s; and third, that the rise of the human-interest photo story, which is the heart of the picture magazine as we know it today, was modeled on European prototypes. While there is no doubt that the German, French, and English pictorial press influenced the rise of an illustrated press in the United States, Hine developed the photo story decades before it appeared in *Vu* and *Die Berliner Illustrirte Zeitung*, and also another unique combination of photos and text that he named "Time Exposures." Finally, it was with a cumbersome 4x5 or 5x7 inch reflex camera called the Graflex that he made his pictures.

Hine fostered an aesthetic as a social or documentary photographer when such terms did not exist. The eminent photohistorian Beaumont Newhall, writing of Hine's work in the March 1938 issue of *Parnassus*, noted that the term "documentary" was not in common currency until 1926. It appeared in the *New York Sun* on February 8, 1926, when "John Grierson spoke of [Robert] Flaherty's film *Moana* as a documentary." Newhall claims that within a year the term was applied to describe still pictures made to illustrate social conditions.

Today, it is a sign of a photojournalist's integrity to struggle with art directors and editors over the design or layout of a photo story. Countless legends abound regarding W. Eugene Smith's battles at *Life*, for example, in this respect. While Hine was not the only working photojournalist in his day, he set precedents in controlling the dissemination of his work.

At *Charities and the Commons* he collaborated with Paul Kellogg on the editing, design, cropping, and copy-writing of photographs and text. At the National Child Labor Committee his work appeared in many different types of printed matter, including pamphlets, leaflets, bulletins, and journals. As a matter of fact, he first referred to his reorganization of pictures and text as a photo story in 1914, nearly eight years after he had developed the idea in the Committee's literature.

The works reintroduced in this book are photographs Hine made in Europe from June 1918 through April 1919. In the spring of 1918, Hine had journeyed to Paris where he was commissioned to make photographs of overseas relief programs of the American Red Cross. During that same period he traveled in northern and southern France and made numerous images of wartime life. Later on, in November 1918, he was a member of a special relief team that traveled to the Balkans. He returned to Paris in late January of the following year, and within the following three months accompanied a smaller group on a tour of northern France and Belgium. In total he made between 1,300 and 1,500 prints and negatives. Subsequently, his photographs were reproduced in the Progressive press and in Red Cross fund-raising material. The photo stories that appeared in *The Survey* about reconstruction and postwar peace offer an enlarged vision of photography and addressed an international theme of "common emancipation."

While members of the photo community have alluded to this work, in fact, this book features the first representative selection of Hine's European photographs. The American Red Cross, which held the material (now on deposit at the Library of Congress) until 1944, had devised a highly eccentric coding and filing system that prevented any researcher, scholar, or librarian from separating out Hine's materials from other photographers'. At the invitation of George Hobart, Curator of Photography at the Library of Congress, I went to Washington to try to crack the cataloguing code, which I did in August 1981, identifying several hundred photographs and negatives. However, prints in this book originate from two other public collections as well: the International Museum of Photography at George Eastman House in Rochester, New York, and the Historical Photo Collection of the United Methodist Church, Commission on Archives and History, in Madison, New Jersey.

The story of how I came to "crack" the Red Cross cataloguing code begins in the fall of 1980. At that time I was directing a photo collection of 177,000 secular and religious, national and international prints owned by the United Methodist Church. Prior to my time a photographer affiliated with the church's audiovisual department had discovered a cache of about two hundred Hine photographs. He contacted Newhall, who confirmed that a group of the American albums did indeed contain "several hundred formerly inaccessible" prints by Hine, but he did not identify which albums these were. Aware that the Methodist repository housed a new group of Hine's photographs, I was sensitive to the possibility that other historical work might emerge.

While there are no records of any financial transactions between the Hine Photo Company and what was then known as the Methodist–Episcopal Church's Audio-Visual Department, Hine apparently had sold prints to the department during his lean years in the 1920s. The church's administrative offices were located on New York's Fifth Avenue near East 22nd Street, an area of Manhattan where social service organizations such as the National Child Labor Committee and the Charities Organization Society had their headquarters.

When the administrative offices of the church were moved in the 1960s, the photo albums were put into storage. My first responsibility was to transfer the photographs and survey them at the department's new offices. Most of the prints pertained to mission-related work in the United States and around the world from 1880 through the 1920s. The repository contained a significant number of documentary, commercial, and artistic photographs that reflected the church's commitment to the "social gospel," or social reform. Indeed, while the sentiment of the American public during the "roaring twenties" nullified the inherent idealism of the Progressive era, the Methodists were still engaged in programs for the indigent and needy. Photographs were used in publications and lantern slide shows to depict the hospitals, orphanages, and schools for women and minorities that they established. In this way the Methodists were simultaneously able to publicize their activities and generate increased support.[1]

Originally stored in large wooden crates, the photographs were collected into 207 albums arranged under international headings, including "India," "China," "Africa," "Europe," and national ones, such as "Cities," "Frontier," etc. The albums contained the work of both overseas missionary photographers and prominent "secular" photographers.

One of the eight albums marked "Europe" ("Europe No. 7") held special interest for me. As a devoted Italophile I was delighted to see that it contained successive pages of photographs of twentieth-century Italy. Yet, what I viewed was not picturesque topographic, architectural, or genre studies associated with Italian photography but wartime photographs. An overwhelming number of the pictures showed bedraggled children who managed to muster a convincing smile for the photographer. These kids distinctly resembled the street urchins who appeared in so many of Hine's Lower East Side and child labor pictures, but I did not make the association at the time.

Given the prevailing subject orientation of the system, the identity of the photographer was not indicated. However, the prints contained a positive etching in the lower-left-hand corner in which an "X" or "W" code and a one to three digit number appeared.

Like their American counterparts, the Italian children emerge as poignant and enduring survivors. Nearly all of them are shown working, although the "feel" of the pictures is often playful. Other photos showed trucks unloading clothing, but the American Red Cross insignia is not evident. Beneath each photograph was a descriptive caption in perfect Gregg penmanship indicating the name of a town or the person pictured. In addition to the photographs of Italy, there were scores taken in Serbia and Greece. While the photographer's name was not supplied, it was clear from the subject grouping of the pictures and their style that these photographs were made by a single photographer. There was a consistency to their signature and "intentionality" that signaled a serious photographer at work. With their people-oriented content, they evoked a compassionate, humane quality unusual for wartime images. In total there were 122 images of Italy and the Balkans in the album.

In examining other albums labeled "Europe" I discovered an additional seventy-six photographs of France and Belgium. Again, they appeared on successive pages and had a stylistic resemblance to one another. The exact sites of these photographs were more difficult to identify unless there was some reference, e.g., a sign in Flemish, in the picture. While the captions provided some information about the town pictured (which may no longer exist), there was no identification of the photographer. Learning that the "entry books" that would have supplied this data had disappeared, I decided that it was imperative to find out who made these photographs, when they were done, and for what purpose. I committed many of them to memory and began to search out their origin. I engaged in a campaign to track down everyone associated with the audio-visual department to see if their recollections might be helpful.

After I had spent months reviewing pictorial histories of World War I for traces of the mystery photographer, my superior at the

Methodist offices, Betty Thompson, happened to give me a book by Judith Mara Gutman entitled *Lewis Hine and the American Social Conscience*. The monograph contains a long introductory text and a portfolio section of Hine's work that spans his lifetime. Among the pictures in the one-hundred-page folio section was a group identified as coming from Hine's "lost" European work, done during and after World War I. Amidst these photographs I recognized one of the "mystery" photos from the Methodist collection; the photographer of the "Methodist" pictures must have been Lewis Hine.

Gutman's text noted that the photographs reproduced were largely selected from the archives at the International Museum of Photography at George Eastman House, but that the bulk of Hine's European work was to be found in the American Red Cross Collection at the Library of Congress. (Gutman had turned up a handful of pictures at the Library with Hine's name typed onto a cataloguing label on the verso of the print.) Her text explained that Hine's photographs and negatives at the Library had been catalogued in an obscure manner, and that she had not been able to isolate them. She estimated that among the 100,000 items in the collection there must have been 1,000 Hine negatives and photographs.

Immediately I telephoned George Hobart to advise him of the discovery of the Methodist Hine prints and to make an appointment to work with the Library's materials. He confirmed that in the fourteen years since Gutman's book was published no one had solved the mystery of Hine's American Red Cross prints and negatives. He was, however, delighted to learn about the church's collection and invited me to have a go at deciphering the code. Armed with contact prints of the 198 Hine/Methodist photos, I arrived in Washington to begin work.

Transferred to the Library's Prints and Photographs Division in 1944, as with most collections of old photographs, the American Red Cross Collection was originally catalogued by the librarian who accessioned it. At the time, no one was aware that his coding system was so puzzling. When he died, he took the code and information about the collection with him.

The materials that I worked with included prints, negatives, and data cards: there were no manuscript documents at the Library. The organization of the collection is as follows: Each American Red Cross print is affixed to a piece of posterboard that measures about 10x12 inches. The verso of the board contains a cataloguing label; a carbon copy of this label is affixed to the data cards. Unfortunately, the name of the photographer usually does not appear, but a caption, a Red Cross subject heading, and the date the photograph was made are supplied.

The second part of the collection consists of about 50,000 negatives arranged not by national heading but by letter codes, such as "A," "B," "X," and "W." Many of the negatives represent images that do not correspond to existing photographs. Each negative was also given a number, such as "W1." The negatives were stored in individual enclosures with a code stamped on the outside of each envelope but no caption information.

The third part of the collection consists of data cards that conform to the same letter–numerical code cataloguing system as the negatives. The cards also duplicate the information that appears on the verso of the mounted prints. Again, neither credit for the photograph nor the negative number is usually provided. Other pieces of information such as the source, a thematic classification, country, number, and date are inconsistently supplied.

After reviewing what was known, Hobart and I boarded an elevator that took us to one of the Library's huge, underground storage areas. He then ushered me from one end of the room to the other—a space of several thousand square feet—relating information he had gleaned over the years. I nodded appreciatively, listening all the while for some clue that would connect our research, but nothing emerged that seemed remotely related. At some point we completed our journey and stood silently gazing at the rows of file cabinets that constituted our promised land.

Our next step was to examine the Methodist prints. As I have already mentioned, etched onto the bottom-left- and/or right-hand corner was a letter–numerical code. Pointing to this "X" and "W" designation I asked Hobart if there was a file cabinet with "X" negatives, since the geographic arrangement of the prints was not useful to our search. We walked to one of the file cabinet drawers that contained negatives. It bore no exterior label. I slowly pulled out the bottom drawer and noticed that the first negative envelope had an "X" stamped onto its outside flap. Taking the contact print I had identified from Gutman's book, I compared it with the "X" negative. Voila! The print matched the negative. We later found the "W" drawer and discovered that there, too, we could match contact prints to negatives. In short, the "X" photographs and negatives pertained to Hine's work in Italy and the Balkans, the "W" photographs to France and Belgium.[2]

I was immediately invited to curate a show of Hine's European prints, and over the next three years I worked intermittently to isolate all of his photos and negatives. In November 1984, the traveling exhibition, *Lewis Hine in Europe: 1918–19*, opened at the Baruch Gallery in New York.

The breakdown of the European materials is as follows: The Library of Congress, which is custodian of the entire American Red Cross collection of 50,000 prints and 50,000 negatives, holds the largest number of Hine's European photographs and negatives. It also contains thousands of wartime-relief photographs of nurses administering to injured soldiers and the handicapped, orphaned, or sick children of France, but it is virtually impossible to determine which are Hine's. The Library holds 106 Balkan Survey, or "X" coded, 4x5 inch negatives and 340 prints. Of the "W" or Reconstruction photographs, twelve prints exist in the Red Cross collection as well as 141 5x7 inch negatives. George Eastman House holds the second largest group of Hine's European work, including wartime images that were made in France throughout the spring and summer of 1918 (prior to the Balkan Survey). The photographs contain merely a four-digit code that, like the Balkan Survey prints, does not follow chronologically, so that prints catalogued in the "2000s" and "7000s" pertain to the same period. In total, George Eastman House is custodian of 540 wartime and postwar "X" and "W" prints and negatives.[3] The collection of the Methodist Commission on Archives and History does not contain any negatives but includes 122 prints from the Balkan Survey and 76 from the Reconstruction or Special Survey. Finally, a selection of 120 Italian and Balkan prints is part of the Floyd and Marion Rinhart Collection at Ohio State University, Columbus, Ohio.

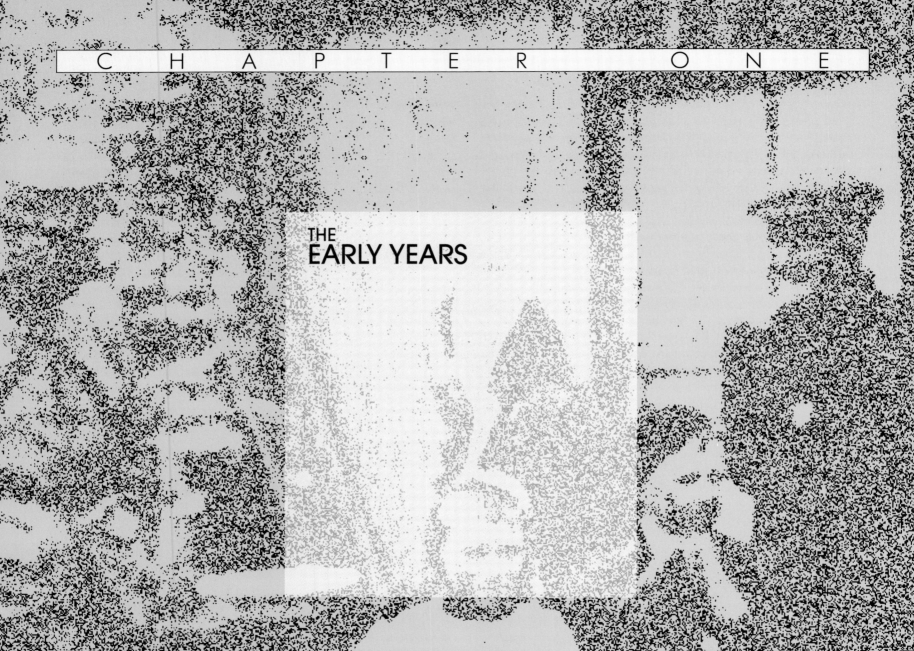

CHAPTER ONE

THE
EARLY YEARS

Lewis Wickes Hine was born in Oshkosh, Wisconsin, on September 26, 1874, to Douglas Hall and Sarah Hayes Hine. His father was an easterner and native of a small, upstate town called Cairo, New York. After spending five years on a coffee plantation in Costa Rica, he settled his family in the Midwest in 1871. As an older man Lewis Hine jokingly referred to Oshkosh as a "saw dust city," alluding apparently to its prominent lumber industry. There he, the Hines' only son and youngest of three children, grew up.

Little is known about Hine's early family life and years as an adolescent. He left no personal manuscript material that accounts for his activities prior to 1920, with the exception of some family photographs. As a result, historians have been dependent on autobiographical material Hine recounted in the late 1930s —particularly to Beaumont Newhall, then at the Museum of Modern Art, and Elizabeth McCausland, an art critic and photo historian—as well as stories related by family, friends, and colleagues.

As a result, monographs about Hine have offered conflicting facts about his pre–New York years. One account, for example, attributed Hine's early visual influences to his father's sign-writing business, although in conversations conducted by McCausland in 1938 in preparation for a major catalogue essay, he did not mention his father in that context. (Hine did indicate that his father owned a coffee shop and restaurant until 1890.) One important fact that we *can* ascertain is that Hine did not set out to be a photographer.

Hine's coming of age occurred in 1892, the year his sixty-three-year-old father was accidentally killed. Lewis had just grad-

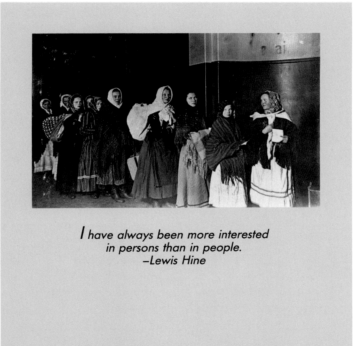

I have always been more interested in persons than in people.
–Lewis Hine

uated from high school. While one sister was already married, and the other, Lola, was gainfully employed as a local elementary school teacher, Hine assumed the role of "man of the house" and found full-time work in an upholstery factory. There he was initiated into the rigors of sweatshop work; he labored thirteen-hour days, six days a week at a weekly salary of four dollars.

From the beginning, Hine was interested in art, particularly wood sculpture. After his father's death, he worked at a series of menial jobs, both in factories and retail stores. Simultaneously, he attended the State Normal School, which featured a type of university extension program. There he took classes in sculpture, drawing, and stenography—a skill that no doubt came in handy during investigative field trips for the National Child Labor Committee.

A picture of the young Hine moves into focus and serves as a profile of Hine the man: diffident though not timid, serious though a perpetual punster, self-effacing but confident. In his conversations with McCausland, Hine referred to himself during this period as an "ugly duckling," but photographs depict a young man of delicate and somewhat impish beauty. Nevertheless, Hine attracted the attention of Dr. Frank Manny, professor of education and psychology at the State Normal School. (Figure 1) While Hine later claimed to have been "discovered" by him, the fact that Hine was not a student of Manny's suggests that Hine probably sought him out.

By that time, Hine had "risen up the ranks" to become "supervising sweeper" in a local bank. "Dr. Manny" (as he continued to address his mentor throughout their relationship) encouraged

F I G U R E 1

Dr. Frank Manny "discovered" Lewis Hine while he was a student
at the State Normal School in Oshkosh, Wisconsin, urging him
to study education. In 1901 Manny became principal of the
Ethical Culture School in New York and hired Hine as assistant
teacher of nature study and geography. Later, Manny suggested
that they together photograph immigrants at Ellis Island. (GEH)

him to pursue courses in education. In 1900 Hine left Oshkosh and
enrolled in the University of Chicago, where it is believed he studied special education with John Dewey and Ella Flagg Young,
two of the nation's prominent and polemical educators. He remained in Chicago until August 1901.

In the summer of 1901 Manny was appointed superintendent
(principal) of the Ethical Culture School in New York, a private
institution whose student body consisted of mainly first-generation
Jewish immigrant children. Manny invited several Normal School
teachers and Hine to join the faculty. At a starting salary of $425 a
year, Hine assumed the job of "polishing brains at the Ethical
Informary" as assistant teacher of nature study and geography.

The Ethical Culture Society was instrumental in developing
a series of unique educational programs designed for the new
immigrants populating New York. Founded by Felix Adler, a moral-
ist, philosopher, and reformer, the Society opened the first Free
Kindergarten and established a Workingman's School with a first
and second grade.

In the decades prior to 1901, an unprecedented wave of
northern and southeastern European immigrants entered the United
States. Their ports of entry and processing, Castle Garden, New
York, in the 1890s and later Ellis Island, brought millions of families
into New York City, where many eventually settled. Immigrants
were frequently ushered into textile factories on New York's Lower
East Side, and into steel mills in Pittsburgh, where they emerged
as a cheap labor force in the industrial workplace. Nationally,
however, anti-immigrant sentiment rose proportionately with the
arrival of more and more "foreigners."

The Ethical Culture School emerged as a progressive institution that represented a way for "successful immigrants" to
Americanize their children. Its philosophy was partly modeled on
principles espoused by the Transcendentalists, and it emphasized
development of human values like individualism as well as the
instilling of a firm sense of community responsibility. As Howard
Radest, current director of the Ethical Culture Schools, explained,
its courses were drawn from a vision of "experience and learning
as a sacred text."

In many ways the school represented an ideal job opportunity for Lewis Hine. Its curriculum embraced John Dewey's innovative educational program and the ideals of the Progressive
Movement, which stressed the social origin of economic and
political issues.

Unlike other schools of the era, it offered courses in both
academic subjects and trade skills such as handiwork, art, weav-
ing, shop, and, in 1904, photography. Later on, Hine apparently
also took advantage of the school's strong commitment to printing and graphic arts, and as early as 1906 began designing
printed matter for the National Child Labor Committee—an organization that Dr. Adler co-founded. Indeed, Adler envisioned the
school as ". . . intended to contribute to the solution of the great
social problems by means of a profound reformation of the system
of education." (L.C.) And, in terms of furthering Hine's initial procliv-

ities, Radest has clarified that it was conceived as a nonvocational institution "designed to give special fitness to those who will be artists later on."

It is interesting to speculate on the reasons why Manny chose nature study and geography for Hine to teach, given the considerable acumen he demonstrated in relation to Hine's development. In some ways Hine remained the perennial innocent whose personal values were rooted in a traditional midwestern upbringing. Independent, moral, and optimistic, Hine was imbued in his early days in the big city with a deep love of nature, one that he enjoyed sharing with his students. In 1904, for example, when he began teaching photography, some of the class's first field trips were to parks in the city. There the students would make landscape photographs that he would later use in instructing them about "silhouetting."

Yet, Hine was a complex man who challenged himself and the world around him. One of his first published articles appeared in the *Oshkosh Northwestern* in October 1903, and it reveals a boyish charm unusual in a thirty-year-old man—a charm Hine would employ to good advantage. Writing of a trip to the Catskill Mountains outside of New York City, he noted:

> I spent the night above the clouds and awoke in the morning to an experience new to me. It was a clear, sunny day, with bright, blue sky overhead. Below, shutting off entirely the view of the lower country, was a mass of white cumulus clouds stretching away to the horizon and looking like a great tempestuous sea. . . .

Hine added that even Rip Van Winkle appeared, ". . . or almost for at any crackling of the bushes one turns, half expecting to see the old bent form. . . ."

The ideal landscape evoked in this piece reflects a curious portrait of Hine, one both wholesome and whimsical. The finely veiled quality of "corniness" that is evident would appear in his work intermittently prior to 1920 but with greater frequency in his postwar years. Nevertheless, perhaps it was his purity that motivated him to celebrate the ordinary man, woman, and child. Certainly, Hine's whimsy enabled him to connect with children, who constitute some of his strongest photographs.

This piece also demonstrates a decided literary flair, which Hine cultivated as he began to write passionately about the value of photography as an art form. These early articles also reveal a sophisticated insight into the properties of the photograph. And, in his work for the National Child Labor Committee, he was engaged in a prodigious output of reports, lectures, and articles. He also wrote a children's book about his experiences as an "investigator with a camera."

At an undetermined point during his second year at the school, 1903–04, Dr. Manny approached Hine to assume the position of school photographer and to document classroom activities. Although Hine had never handled a camera, Manny clarified his choice many years later: "I had long wanted to use the camera for records and you [were] the only one who seemed to see what I was after."

Hine, whose youthful aspirations had included becoming a sculptor or painter, took on his new position with characteristic alacrity. He rigorously studied photochemistry and read both amateur and professional "how-to" magazines. His first camera, and the one he continued to use, was a 5x7 Graflex. At the outset of his career Hine also employed a "rickety" tripod and, for nighttime photographs or interior studies, flashpowder (a compound of magnesium and an accelerator) and a "t" bar, "a horizontal pan on a vertical hollow rod with a plunger," into which the compound was placed.

The most important feature of the Graflex was that, as a single-lens reflex camera, it enabled a photographer to pre-visualize a photograph, though the image that appeared on the ground glass was inverted left to right. It was advertised as "the inimitable camera," which provided "pictures as you see them, while you see them, and at the desired moment."

Hine's earliest photographs, some of which still exist in the archives of the school, depict boys studiously engaged in woodworking activities, girls in long dresses elaborately executing the latest modern dance movement, and both busily engaged in science labs. Hine's quick success in mastering photography resulted in his selection by Manny to teach it in 1904. It was during this period that Hine produced a body of landscapes, with and without his students.

These earliest photographs bear little resemblance to the direct, frontal portraits that were to become his trademark. Rather, they are heuristic devices that coupled the study of photography with a related subject, or topical studies of school life. On a "Commerce Camera Club" excursion, for example, Hine noted that the children were familiarized with the "ins and outs of his or her camera" in addition to making pictures "pertinent to their study of commerce." (Figure 2)

Hine wrote several articles about photography that were accompanied by both his photographs and those of his students. The articles treated the importance of photography as an educational tool, and outlined principles that were to govern Hine's

own aesthetic commitment to the medium throughout his lifetime. In a departure from standard photographic practice, Hine joined the social (i.e., "storytelling") possibilities of the photograph with the artistic ones.

> If more of the beginners in photography could realize that the highest aim of the artist is to have something to relate and to know how to select the right things to reproduce that story by accenting the important parts and minimizing the effects of the unimportant factors, they would be willing to spend sometime in the preparation for the quest of that pot of gold at the end of the photographer's rainbow—the artistic photograph.
>
> (*The Photographic Times*, p. 490, Nov. 1906)

Of course, in the period that Hine was teaching photography he was also learning it himself. Rather than emphasizing the acquisition of technical skills, Hine treated the camera not as a deus ex machina but as an instrument. His knowledge of the camera as a technical apparatus, while sufficient, was never his priority. His method consisted of "just doing it" and reading about the latest chemical and technical advances. The same may be said about his relationship to his photographic prints. By 1908, in addition to printing his own work, he established a photo processing and printing business out of his home in Yonkers, which he called the Hine Photo Company.[4]

In 1904 Hine produced his "first bullseye with craftsmen," a portrait of the school's printing instructor entitled "The Printer." (Figure 3) Twenty years later Hine would credit this photograph as the inspiration for his series of "work portraits." In a chiaroscuro rendering atypical of Hine's signature, the scene is charged with a mystical drama: a white-haired artisan, fully absorbed in his craft, is illuminated by a gleaming beam of white light. The photograph has a painterly quality reminiscent of the Italian High Renaissance masters.

In his early articles Hine often referred to painting and was dependent on it as a point of departure for studying composition. In his Ellis Island portraits, made later that year, and the tenement

F I G U R E 2

Hine began teaching photography in 1904. In this illustration he is pictured with his Ethical Culture School students on a Commerce Camera Club excursion to the freight terminal in South Brooklyn. (NYPL)

homework series, made on New York's Lower East Side, he would refer to Raphael's *Madonna of the Chair* to illustrate "the salient features of a good picture." He reiterated the relationship of art and photography in an article entitled "Photography in the School":

> The fundamental aim of the course is to help the pupils to a better appreciation of good photography and how to attain it,—in short, to give the artist's point of view, for, in the last analysis, good photography is a question of art.
>
> (*The Photographic Times*, p. 230, Aug. 1908)

The year 1904 emerges as a watershed in Hine's personal and professional life. He briefly returned to Oshkosh to marry Sara Ann Rich, a local elementary school teacher he apparently met while attending the State Normal School, and they returned east to New York. Eventually they settled in Yonkers, a town outside of New York City, where they lived until 1917. Later in 1904, at the suggestion of Dr. Manny, the two men journeyed to Ellis Island. Manny's decision was motivated by several factors, including the xenophobic fervor rampant throughout the country, the eastern European backgrounds of many of his students, and a historical link he recognized between families who fled England in the seventeenth century because of religious persecution and immigrants who fled pogroms in the late nineteenth century.

Years later Mrs. Hine would add that Hine's interest in accompanying Manny evolved out of conversations she and her husband had with friends. Hine himself would attribute his desire to photograph immigrants, in conversations with Elizabeth McCausland, to "news value" and "humanitarian interest." Nonetheless, the urge to photograph "foreigners" was unprecedented during a time when photographers avoided making social images.

From 1903 to 1913 some 10,000,000 immigrants entered the United States—representing about one-tenth of the nation's population. On their initial trip, Hine and Dr. Manny "elbowed [their] way through the crowd," and used gesture and sign language to convey a desire to photograph a person or group. Manny acted as Hine's "caddy." While Hine busied himself with the labors of camerawork and charismatically engaged his subject, Manny functioned as Hine's lighting assistant. He spread the magnesium powder on the "t" bar (which he also held) and in synchronism

F I G U R E   3

Hine referred to this work portrait of the Ethical Culture School's printing instructor, made in 1904, as his "first bullseye" with a camera. (GEH)

with Hine's countdown ignited the powder when Hine tripped the shutter.

The Ellis Island photographs of individuals set a standard for Hine's prewar signature: they are frontal, posed, and direct. In this respect as well, his style countered fin-de-siècle photographic codes, where photographers avoided a frontal style of portraiture because of its aggressive nature. Yet, by focusing on an individual's wan expression, or an archetypal mother–child relationship, Hine made his subjects appear accessible. Cultural differences are subtly evident in the twist of a scarf or cut of a suit; there are both vulnerability and dignity in people's expressions that invite rather than intimidate the viewer.

Pictorially, Hine pursued several strategies. By selecting individuals waiting alone in large empty rooms he made his photographs evoke a compassion that reflects Whitman's lyrical credo, "I am the mate and companion for people." Some face the camera with amused conviction; others—tired and scared—shyly withdraw from the photographer's gaze. His touching portraits of families, whose entire belongings are casually lumped at their feet, encourage a shared feeling of loss and hope.

Hine began working as a photographer nearly twenty years after the amateur photo boom made possible by George Eastman's invention of the small, hand-held Brownie camera. While Kodak emphasized the simplicity with which its product could be used—"You Press the Button, We Do the Rest"—the Graflex was a professional's camera. An examination of its operation may be useful in understanding just how skillful Hine was in producing a photograph under difficult conditions.

Using the camera involved several complicated steps, which may imply the necessity for Hine to pose his subjects. First, he would set the mirror to focus his subject. This was done by opening the aperture to a wide-enough setting so that adequate light would fall on the mirror and be reflected onto the ground glass. Once the subject was focused, then the mirror had to be cocked back into "shooting" position and the correct aperture selected. Second, Hine would choose a shutter speed determined by his reading of existing light. He would turn the "shutter tension" knob, with readings from 1 to 6, to its correct position. The shutter speed would also determine the position of the slit-width gauge, a setting that varied from 0, 1/8, 3/4, to 1 3/4.

The 5x7 camera featured a wide-angle, rectilinear lens with a focal length of about 180mm. Given this lens, the closest Hine could stand to a subject and have him in crisp focus was about four feet. The size of the lens also affects the depth of field available; the larger the lens the less there is. Also, as the aperture increases in size, the background becomes less sharp. (The larger the "f" stop number, the smaller the opening.) As a result, Hine's photographs have plenty of foreground detail while the background fades out into a fuzzy blur. In Hine's early pictures, where the emphasis was to render the subject "close-up," this background blurriness created a desirable effect. It placed the subject within a larger context, one easily recognizable, but not distracting to the foreground action.

Although the Graflex itself was not especially heavy—it weighed between 18 and 20 pounds—Hine's technical baggage included an assortment of glass negatives and holders, flash-powder and "t" bar, and a wooden tripod. The glass negatives were stored inside a leather pouch that hung from his shoulder and held about twelve plates. In his years of investigative field-work, Hine—a self-defined "featherweight"—had as much as fifty pounds of equipment to carry.

The camera's body was rugged and compact, almost cubical, and, considering the solid materials of which it was made, relatively light. Its rectilinear lens was about eight inches long and uncoated. Thus, if Hine took a picture on a bright or sunny day its sky was almost always entirely devoid of cloud details and bleached out. Shutter speeds varied from 1/10 to 1/1,000 of a second.

The Graflex used pre-coated glass plates or negatives that were placed into wooden holders that fit on the back of the camera, each containing two negatives. Once a picture was composed and focused, the shade on the holder was pulled out so that the negative was ready for exposure. After the shutter was pressed, the photographer would reinsert the shade into the negative holder, wind the slit-width of the shutter back to its previous position, pull out the holder, and turn it around for the next picture.

Thus, the production of sequential photographic images was not a nonstop process but a quick execution by a skilled photographer of the proper motions.

Due to the slowness of the film emulsion and lens, making photographs in low-light (interior) or nighttime situations necessitated the use of flashpowder, also known as "blitzlightpulver." The burst of light provided a more expedient method of producing a picture than long exposures, which required the subject to remain still. Although in isolated cases Hine may have used both the time exposure mechanism as well as flashpowder to produce an on-site action photograph of children laboring indoors, flashpowder was more frequently used to make low-light photographs. Given the volatile nature of flashpowder, the use of artificial light was an acquired skill.

Technically, there were drawbacks to using flashpowder. If a photographer was working with a tripod, one hand needed to be free to hold the flash pan. If one did not use a tripod, a partner would be required. Though only a small amount of magnesium powder was necessary to produce an illuminating flash, the chemical was a highly explosive substance. It produced both a loud bang—hence the term "shooting" a picture—and clouds of voluminous smoke. In addition, the smoke would make it uncomfortable for the subject to remain in the room, let alone sit or stand in the same place for subsequent exposures. And, after a few flashes, the "t" bar itself would become very hot, so that magnesium added too soon to the "t" bar would automatically ignite. This made the production of photographs an even trickier operation for the inexperienced photographer.

In the Ellis Island portraits, Hine had a partner. While the spectacle of making a photograph had its own entertainment value, there was also a certain amount of danger involved. A photographer risked losing parts of fingers if he did not remove his hand quickly enough after igniting the flashpowder, or singeing his hair, which Hine admitted doing many times while photographing at Ellis Island.

Later on he worked the camera and flash alone. After approaching a person or group, demonstrating an interest in photographing them, arranging them carefully, and returning to his position by the camera, he found that:

> Meantime, the group had strayed around a little and you had to give a quick focal adjustment, while someone held the lamp. The shutter was closed, of course, plateholder inserted and cover-slide removed. Usually,—the lamp retrieved and then the real work began. By that time most of the group was either silly or stony or weeping with hysteria because the bystanders had been busy pelting them with advice. . . . and the climax came when you raised the flashpan aloft over them and they waited, rigidly, for the blast. It took all the resources of a hypnotist, a supersalesman, and a ball pitcher to prepare them to play the game and then to outguess them so most were not either wincing or shutting eyes when the time came to shoot. (A.A.A.)

While it may be difficult to comprehend the inherent boldness of Hine's photographs, for an aspiring turn-of-the-century photographer the social stigma associated with immigrants rendered the subject matter virtually taboo. In addition to a lack of positive information on the topic in the popular press, progressive magazines also limited their coverage.[5] With the connotation of "foreigner" or "other," popular and intellectual myths about immigrants proliferated, harping on their uncleanliness (they lived in unventilated, small tenements), illiteracy (they could not read, write, or speak English), and ethnicity (they were unresponsive to American cultural values).

Of course, Hine was not the first photographer cum social reformer to direct his camera at people in need. In the nineteenth century, Thomas Annan made pictures of the streets of Glasgow, Scotland, and John Thomson and Paul Martin portrayed working-class men and women in England. In America, the Danish immigrant Jacob Riis is probably best known for the first studies of New York's indigent. Certainly, Riis created an audience for Hine's reformist imagery. Nevertheless, Riis's strategy and working method may be contrasted with Hine's. For, on close examination, Riis actually perpetuated the very myths he sought to repudiate.

A police reporter for the *New York Evening Sun*, Riis was assigned to the East End, the point of Manhattan's Lower East Side where the Mulberry Bend took a sharp angle. Keenly aware of the wretched conditions Italian families endured there, he set out to describe their plight in his columns. Upon discovering that his stories did not sufficiently arouse public anger over this issue, he decided to use a camera to record the poverty in vivid detail.

Although Riis is often credited as both photographer and caption writer, in fact, he did not photograph many of his subjects. Rather, he directed two amateur photographers, Henry G. Piffard and Richard Hoe Lawrence. By employing a less volatile version of the original "blitzlightpulver" formula, they made some of the first interior photographs in the United States.[6]

Riis was proud of his achievement at having attained the status of an "assimilated American." When he set out to counter public opinion about immigrants, one fiction that he contested was that foreigners were "unclean." Nevertheless, "dirt" emerges as an overriding visual motif in many of the photographs his name is associated with. "Five Cents Lodging, Bayard Street," for example, a photograph converted into a line drawing for his pioneering book, *How the Other Half Lives: Studies Among the Tenements of New York*, shows a handful of men inside a filthy flophouse room. The men are in two beds and barely visible in the photograph, but enough generic detail can be registered to read their inherent "foreignness"—they are dark and swarthy. The camera is focused on foreground details of the room itself: work shoes stand prominently in the corner of the frame amidst the disorder of rumpled clothes and dirty blankets, walls, and satchels.

While Riis's photographs serve as brutal testimony to the deplorable conditions immigrants and the poor endured, they did not encourage identification with the people depicted but distanced the viewer from them. Indeed, Riis's subjects appear lazy (they're in bed), dim (the room is lit for the foreground, the men are in the background), and anonymous (they are not identified). They emerge as illustrations—symbolic allusions—to the title of his book, "the *other* half." In addition, Riis's text is replete with accepted racial and ethnic slurs, such as Negroes are "sensual," the Chinese "clean but gamblers," etc.

Riis's ideas were typical of a "charities" mentality common in the late nineteenth century. His program of reform for the Mulberry Bend involved razing the slum and displacing its residents. Nevertheless, Riis received support for his program—the Bend eventually was torn down—and continued his crusade. By the time of his death in 1914 he had published ten books and delivered countless public lectures about poverty.

It is unclear what, if any, relationship Lewis Hine had with Riis. Apparently, Hine was introduced to him by a mutual colleague, Paul Kellogg, associate editor of the Progressive journal *Charities and the Commons*. During the time that Hine began selling pictures to the magazine, Riis became a member of its Advisory Board. He and Kellogg developed a close friendship and frequently took recreational fishing trips together. Despite Hine's celebration of immigrants, Riis obviously endorsed his work since he purchased lantern slides from him that were used in his illustrated lectures.

Beginning with the Ellis Island studies, Hine set out to apply the elements of a vernacular tradition. His writings evoke a Whitmanesque spirit: in an article for the journal *Education*, he wrote of finding "the picturesque and beautiful in the commonplace . . . to make an artistic photograph." His interest in adapting common forms of expression was described in *The Photographic Times* as "a greater appreciation of the beauties to be found on every hand." Later on, he would add that he "was merely changing his educational efforts from the classroom to the world," and that the role of photography was functional or "productive labor."

By the turn of the century, the conversion of photographs into halftones was becoming more popular. Yet, photographs were used primarily as illustrations (much as Jacob Riis used them), and they were dependent on the accompanying text. From the inception of his career, Hine had a growing sense of the new photograph, one that would combine picture and text as a communications tool. There are presentiments of this interdependent relationship in his early writings that appeared in *The Elementary School Journal*: ". . . the photographs taken during the year have become quite indispensable with reinforcing and varying the written explanation. . . ."

With his work at Ellis Island, Hine had an opportunity to implement principles he had written about. He would follow up his immigrant portraits by taking his camera into the streets of Philadelphia, Chicago, Pittsburgh, and New York's ethnic ghetto, the Lower East Side, and he resumed his work in 1926 when immigrant quotas were reinstituted.

In the immigrant studies Hine elevated what was formerly construed as a quotidian drabness into a sign of struggle and pride. His photographs are charged with an emotional intensity that transcends their value as pictorial documents. In fact, they continue to be employed today as icons of America's immigrant heritage. Within the context of Hine's *oeuvre*, these images represent his first group of photographs that posited a new aesthetic of photography.

BUSINESS REPLY MAIL
FIRST CLASS   PERMIT NO. 6778   NEW YORK, NY

POSTAGE WILL BE PAID BY ADDRESSEE

NO POSTAGE
NECESSARY
IF MAILED
IN THE
UNITED STATES

ABBEVILLE PRESS

P.O. Box 5359
F.D.R. Station
New York, NY 10150

CHAPTER TWO

LEWIS HINE
AND
VERNACULAR CULTURE

Lewis Hine's arrival in New York coincided with America's entering an unprecedented phase of development, a booming era of industrialization and urbanization. While New York, Washington, and Pittsburgh were rapidly developing as industrial centers of great wealth, disparities between rich and poor were painfully evident in the rise of ghettos, slums, and tenements that housed an untouchable class of Americans, the urban poor.

Hine's career as a committed photographer began when he set out to translate the experiences of the immigrant in 1904. Yet, the origins of his social vision and that of his immediate environment, the Ethical Culture School, were first articulated more than half-a-century earlier. They may be traced to pre-industrial traditions rooted in the moral landscapes of nineteenth-century New England and the West, where mutual concern for the functional uses of art gave rise to new forms of expression at once individualistic and democratic.

American culture of the nineteenth century was conceived as an idealistic hegemony of spiritual values. Transcendentalists like Ralph Waldo Emerson and Margaret Fuller sought to merge the real and ideal, and believed that all matter, as an extension of God, was fully embodied in the individual of conscience. In addition to positing the unique value of an individual, the Transcendentalists were involved in connecting people into a larger social and political order. Emerson, for example, "intimated of the oneness" of "all individuals." In an address on the "American Scholar" he elucidated the elements of a vision also inherent in Hine's work, one that might be characterized as democratic humanism: "I embrace the common, I explore and sit at the feet of the familiar, the low. Give me insight into today, and you may have the antique and future worlds."

As John Kouwenhoven has observed, the vernacular tradition was "concern[ed] with the value of the individual and the panoramic effort to comprehend a diversity of people and places in specific local and factual terms." Indeed, one might say vernacular principles emerge as a bulwark of the Progressive Movement in their Emersonian reflection of "oneness." While crafts and folk art are common enough associations, vernacular was "inextricably linked to a utilitarian ethic derived from the burgeoning technology."

In the period framed by the advent of Transcendentalism and the closing of the frontier, two artists emerged who seized upon the principles of democratic humanism and integrated them into their personal ideals of the potential of America, Walt Whitman and Mark Twain. In the same way that their writings embody nineteenth-century America, Hine's photojournalistic work was infused with the spirit of the Progressive era. Hine would enlarge the idea of a vernacular type by (literally) picturing the figure they had invoked.

*For some time now I have been "interpreting" the common (middle)-man,-(even as you and I),- and the critics, even the victims themselves, have been rawther [sic] appreciative. I find this line just as much fun as the previous slants on life have been and I think fully as much of a contribution to the gaiety of nations.
—Lewis Hine (1929)*

extension of God, was fully embodied in the individual of conscience. In addition to positing the unique value of an individual, the Transcendentalists were involved in connecting people into a larger social and political order. Emerson, for example, "intimated of the oneness" of "all individuals." In an address on the "American Scholar" he elucidated the elements of a vision also inherent in Hine's work, one that might be characterized as demo-

Whitman was the first American writer to employ the elements of a vernacular style in his poetry. *Leaves of Grass*, his epic, controversial, lifelong project, was first self-published in 1855. His intentions were to filter the experiences of the common man and woman through himself and create a form of writing that reflected the qualities of a true vernacular type. Whitman's gospel of individualism and collectivism was revealed at length in the inimitable free verse of his ebullient *Leaves of Grass*:

> I celebrate myself, and sing myself
> And what I assume you shall assume
> for every atom belonging to me as good
>   belongs to you.

In addition to its unusual use of language, Whitman's audacity lay in proposing an alternative model of the American hero. Like the central character in Hine's street photographs, the new man inhabiting the New World was urban and common. In a sense, the man Whitman celebrated was pictured on the inside cover of *Leaves'* first edition. Facing the title page is an engraved portrait of a bearded man in an open-neck shirt and Panama hat, looking not like a gentleman but a self-assured, mildly cocky laborer, or "one of the roughs." Whitman used an etching of himself both to typify the hero and to identify himself as its creator. (Figure 4)

Twain's controversial novel, *The Adventures of Huckleberry Finn*, was published thirty years after the first edition of *Leaves of Grass*. It originated from the traditions of journalism, specifically newspaper humor, but had more of a documentary thrust than Whitman's poem in its treatment of racism and slavery. The young Huck Finn's "odyssey of individual liberation" is joined with that of his partner, a runaway slave named Jim. In addition to its critical social commentary, the story was conceived on the notion of the journey as a spiritual quest, a physical expedition. Twain enlarged the category of "common people" to include an as-yet-unarticulated perspective, that of a young man. He was the first writer to discover that the personality of a child could be used to project realistic views of society.

Hine's work would fully merge social, political, and artistic concerns first put forth by Whitman and Twain. His special interest and talent in transposing the spirit of children recalls Twain's novels, which, as Tony Tanner has commented, celebrated the child as a "superior witness in the world." Hine's photographs of child workers for the National Child Labor Committee featured children whose outlook paralleled that of Twain's young heroes (though Hine added heroines to his roster). Rather than picturing the workers as victims, Hine empowered them: his kids have an

F I G U R E 4

Walt Whitman's epic poem *Leaves of Grass* was self-published in 1855 and represented one of the first times that a vernacular figure was used as a spokesman in American poetry. Whitman's portrait symbolized his identification with the common man and established his identity as the poem's creator. (NYPL)

innocent strength and wisdom that enable them to survive. And, his National Child Labor Committee captions included the children's own words as testimony on behalf of the movement to legislate laws prohibiting child labor.

Hine's pictorial aesthetic presented a new way of picturing information. By focusing on proud, beautiful, ordinary people, he was able to "illustrate [my] thesis that the human spirit is the big thing after all." His new angle of vision involved introducing a photographic vernacular figure and selecting familiar, slang, or idiomatic expressions for his captions. His language is filled with a passion and immediacy derived, in the case of underage workers, from their own transforming experience.

For Hine as well, the concept of the journey was tantamount to making photographs. From his first trip to Ellis Island, to the tens of thousands of miles he traversed in his twelve years with the National Child Labor Committee, to his grueling journeys for the American Red Cross in Europe, Hine's travels enabled him to construct his own vision of human interconnectedness. His American and European human-interest social photographs are testimony to Whitman's statement, "In all people I see myself."

In a lantern slide lecture presented to his National Child Labor Committee colleagues, Hine addressed the implications of the picture as a gestalt that "speaks a language learned early in the race and in the individual . . . The picture is the language of all nationalities and all ages." In a prolific array of photo stories for the popular and Progressive press, he instinctually developed a new language, one constituted of syntactical parts of photo and text.

ALFRED STIEGLITZ AND THE PHOTO-SECESSION

An understanding of the milieu of turn-of-the-century photography in New York would be incomplete without addressing the role that Alfred Stieglitz played in formulating an American aesthetic that countered Hine's own. In 1903, a year before Lewis Hine made his first photographs at Ellis Island, the premiere issue of *Camera Work* was published. It was founded and edited by Stieglitz, a young American photographer who had been educated in Europe.

Stieglitz initially studied photography in Germany with Hermann Wilhelm Vogel and was later accepted into England's Photographic Society in 1887. His work was singled out by Peter Henry Emerson, a prominent English photographer and exponent of Naturalistic Photography, who awarded him first prize for a picture of "Italian children clustered around a village well." He returned to New York in 1890 where he edited *The American Amateur Photographer*, which subsequently became *Camera Notes* after the Society for Amateur Photographers merged with the New York Camera Club.

With the advent of *Camera Work*, Stieglitz boldly proposed that photography be ascribed equal status to painting and sculpture. In an era that witnessed the proliferation of the photo hobbyist and concomitant repudiation of photography's artistic possibilities, it was the first American journal to present photography as an art form. However, Stieglitz did not look to vernacular culture as the inspiration for his new artistic model. Rather, his theoretical ideas were located within the elitist cultural traditions of the modern art movement in Europe. He championed two types of photographic prints, the Pictorial (altered) and the "straight" (unadulterated).

In fundamental ways, Hine's work, having been inspired by Progressive modernism, had no relationship to the elitist modernism fashioned on the pages of *Camera Work*. While Hine's photographs did conform to the straight picture, his direct, social signature was not appropriate to the formal priorities that Stieglitz espoused. And, while Hine's work was made for the printed page, it was transposed by crude (economical) halftones that emphasized the human, i.e., social, element and obscured any technical highlights in the original print. Stieglitz, on the other hand, insisted on the most advanced technological standards for his innovative art magazine and adopted a panoply of printing processes. These included gravure, mezzotint-gravure, duogravure, hand-toned gravure, halftone, three-color halftone, four-color halftone, and collotype. Visually, the "Pictorialist" original and reproduced photograph conformed to a fin-de-siècle appreciation of beauty and had a soft-focus, ethereal quality reminiscent of Post-Impressionist painting. It is interesting to note that mass-produced photographs sometimes took on the altered, painterly appearance of Stieglitz's artistic images. Even Hine's photographs, for example, manifested the look of Pictorialist photographs after they had been retouched to suit a popular journal's use of them as illustrations.[7]

A fine art magazine, *Camera Work* informed the reader of formal concepts involving representation. In fact, in viewing issues of the journal one would be hard-pressed to find any evidence at all of the spirit of the Progressive era that vitalized America at the time. With the rise of a Pictorialist School, soft-focus renderings of

Alfred Stieglitz was the Photo-Secession's leading spokesman. "The Terminal" is an example of a "straight" photograph. (GEH)

pastoral scenes abounded.[8] Photographs were not, however, unilaterally oriented toward depicting rural life, although there were tacit standards in relation to subject matter as well. Journals offered such strict aesthetic guidelines as "storytelling [is] something unworthy of artistic photography." Nevertheless, these principles were primarily oriented to a privileged class of photographers who exhibited their work in salons. Indeed, with the emphasis on picturesque urban/rural landscapes or idyllic mother–children relationships, this "style" conveniently promoted a vision of America at once homogeneous and idealized. (Figures 5 and 6)

The name that Stieglitz gave this new movement, Photo-Secession, was adopted from the group that launched the mod-

ern art movement in Munich in 1897. *Camera Work* featured American and European photographers under this rubric who were concerned with fulfilling Nietzsche's vision of the artist as a "worshipper of forms, of tones. . . ."

Historically, Stieglitz and Hine emerge as colleagues in the struggle to posit photography as an art and communications form. At that time, however, they had no relationship whatsoever. With Stieglitz's reliance on European cultural values to authorize his campaign, the Photo-Secession reflects a heightened post-Victorian classicism, one that stands in adverse relationship to the Progressive's democratic ideals.

Stieglitz, an urbane, gregarious man, and an incessant

and Robert Demachy—whose work was highlighted in the maga-zine's pages—Stieglitz cultivated a guru-like mystique.

Hine was obviously aware of Stieglitz's efforts at promoting photography and brought his students to view work at the gallery, located at 291 Fifth Avenue. Indeed, one can imagine a nattily dressed but slight Mr. Hine, ever playful in his role as inveterate teacher, ushering in a group of noisy and enthusiastic students to view the august photo-laden walls of Stieglitz's powerhouse—the Little Galleries of the Photo-Secession.[9]

Nevertheless, while Hine did not envision himself as working within the specific artistic parameters of the Photo-Secession he was interested in joining the artistic and social components of the photograph. As we have seen, Hine's early writings addressed the educational function of the photograph and alluded to his own personal aspirations with regard to making "artistic" photographs. But, Hine's artistic impulses would best be channeled into modern-ist experiments with the organization of photographs and text. At this early stage of his work, the display of the photograph as an original work of art, that is, as a salable commodity, was inimical to his strategy of employing reproduced photographs in the ser-vice of social change.

Although Hine's vision may be seen as essentially vernacu-lar in character, he, too, assimilated "high art" concerns in his work. While Hine's photographs may not have manifested a frac-turing of the picture plane (a modernist concern treated exten-sively in the pages of *Camera Work*), the serial nature of the photo story—call it a "fragmentation" of sorts—reflects his own interpretation of modernist issues.

Hine and Stieglitz were each successful in creating a new audience for photography. Their programs were analogous inso-far as each formulated a new vision of photography that, his-torically, was mutually beneficial to the other's. During a time when photographs were viewed as an inferior form of illustration, unable to meet the high criteria of etchings and drawings, Hine pioneered the photo story format. At the same time, Stieglitz's position represented a radical, albeit well-financed gesture to make certain that photography was accepted as a genuine form of artistic expression.

talker, was by all accounts an imposing presence. Devotees of the new photography relied upon his intellectual and aesthetic passion to further the acceptance of photography as an art form. With the financial support of European photographers of inde-pendent wealth and power, like Baron de Meyer, Heinrich Kühn,

CHAPTER THREE

THE KELLOGG BROTHERS AND PROGRESSIVE JOURNALISM

Hine's early accomplishments as a social photographer grew out of Frank Manny's recognition of the photograph's informational potential. Subsequently, while he was still employed as a teacher, Hine met Arthur and Paul Kellogg and began to sell photographs to *Charities and the Commons*, the social welfare magazine they edited. In the decade that he served as its staff photographer the journal emerged as a principal vehicle for their collaborative photo stories about Progressive and postwar issues.

By the turn of the century the country had shifted from a rural to an urban nation. The Progressive agenda reflected this change by focusing on problems affecting the cities. However, the unique aspect of its program was to approach these matters not as local issues, indigenous to a particular city, but as problems affecting the nation as a whole. These included tenement homework, exploitation of women in the work force, poor housing and work conditions for immigrants, and the persistence of child labor. To publicize these issues as well as a growing list of others, the journal effectively utilized a photographic image that contained the by-line "By Lewis W. Hine."

Turn-of-the-century Progressive America was engaged in an important era of social transition: The scientifically trained "social worker" had begun to replace the name and rhetoric associated with the "charities" worker. Concomitantly, social workers emerged as an integral force in urban communities and also became more visible as a cohesive (national) political group. Newly trained to approach their profession with both the acuity of the scientist and the breadth of a

Indeed, the development of social documentary photography is so closely tied to advances in printing technology and the growth of the popular press that the flowering of the movement would be unthinkable without the capability of the halftone process printing plate to transmute silver images into inked print.
—Naomi Rosenblum,
A World History of Photography

humanist, social workers wrote articles and reports about the families they served that reflected an attitude less morally judgmental than that of their predecessors. In addition to the charts, graphs, and statistics employed as illustrations in their printed matter, there was a growing acknowledgment of the value of photographs that dignified human life—Hine's "camera work."

While there had been a tradition in the American press of the impartial journalist as crusader—as, for example, in the work of Jacob Riis—the first decade of this century marked a dramatic transformation in the fabric of the American press. As corporate interests came to nefariously dominate virtually every sphere of society, there was a public outcry as "Big Business" infiltrated government. Vernacular magazines, referred to as "muckraking" journals, investigated and challenged this unbridled materialism in a variety of ways. They published essays that addressed the rising concern about business and political corruption. In addition to their written exposés, these magazines began to combine halftone illustration with contemporaneous news topics, such as conservation, pure food legislation, juvenile delinquency, and tenement housing. By 1903 the Progressive era was born.

Muckraking journals set precedents in photo illustration but they did not make full use of social imagery. One of the earliest, classic corporate exposés, for example, was Ida Tarbell's controversial series of articles on the Rockefeller family and fortune entitled "The History of the Standard Oil Company," which appeared in *McClure's*. The articles included photographic portraits of prominent businessmen and political leaders both to embellish the story and to discredit these men. Later on, in 1906, Lincoln Steffens's article "Ben B. Lindsay: The Just Judge" employed uncredited photographs of delinquent boys.

With the coalition of the popular press and public support, social movements were erected on the hope of revitalizing America's spirit. To succor a growing class of unemployed, unskilled, and impoverished Americans, societies began to form "lend a hand" organizations in the cities. One of the earliest and largest to engage in health and welfare work for deprived persons was the New York Charities Organization Society, founded in 1881. In light of the changes sweeping the nation and the press, the Society asked its secretary, Edward T. Devine, to edit a more contemporary version of its journal, which catered to an "old-fashioned" case-worker sensibility that viewed poverty as a result of individual failings. The journal was appropriately called *Charities*.

In addition to editing the journal, Devine founded the New York Summer School of Philanthropy, which was subsequently referred to as the New York School of Philanthropy affiliated with Columbia University, and later became the Columbia University Graduate School of Social Work. The School attracted aspiring social workers throughout the country. Paul Kellogg, a young, blond-haired, blue-eyed, idealistic reporter from Kalamazoo, Michigan, enrolled there in 1902. Devine "discovered" Kellogg and offered him a job as assistant editor of *Charities*.

Kellogg subsequently hired his older brother Arthur as second assistant editor. Arthur, a tall, dark-haired, bespectacled man, was the practical and managerial member of the team. He, too, attended the Columbia School of Social Work where he met a fellow student, Lewis Hine, in 1904. Apparently, the older Kellogg and Hine—being somewhat closer in age—became friends. In fact, it was Arthur who suggested to him that he become a "sociological photographer," a codified term that meant a photographer of child workers. Soon after, Hine heeded Arthur's advice by pursuing free-lance work for the fledgling National Child Labor Committee. As early as 1907 his first photo stories were published by the Committee, although the photographs appear to have been made in the summer and fall of 1906. (See Chapter Four.) Trained as an educator, Hine brought to photography both

visual and textual skills. At a time when professional photographers eschewed pictures that told a story and opted for artistic photographs in which technique dominated content, Hine inverted the paradigm. Interested in coupling the ideals of the artist with the strategies of a scientist he was a perfect Progressive photographer. Just as his Ellis Island photographs positively focused attention on working-class individuals, he pioneered socially related subject matter as a new domain of photography. Thus, his pictures compounded photographic meaning: in addition to representing people, they imparted a point-of-view that gave the "average" and professional reader an opportunity to see the poor not as inferior people or—as Hine put it—"not a lower form of life."

As Frank Manny guided Hine to new and broader horizons, so did the Kelloggs. Through hard work, teamwork, imagination, and daring, the two editors and photographer would focus on the capabilities of the photograph to convey news of social welfare issues. In addition, the Kelloggs introduced Hine to leading Progressives whose values were allied with his own, such as Florence Kelley of the National Consumer's League, the socialist John Spargo, Owen Lovejoy of the National Child Labor Committee, Lillian Wald of the Henry Street Settlement, and Homer Folks of the State Charities Aid Association—each of whom would emerge as a colleague during his career. In 1931 Hine wrote to the brothers:

> . . . I want to tell you that I shall always remember what a factor you two and *Survey* has [sic] been in putting my stuff on the map, to say nothing of what your appreciation and encouragement have meant all through the first quarter century of Hineography. The other three quarters ought to be that much easier. I am convinced that had the Paul–Art cooperation failed to synchronize at various critical periods I might still be polishing brains at the Ethical Informary so, please, for them and for me accept my heartfelt thanks. (S.W.H.A.)

Charities offered new possibilities for the dissemination of Hine's work, and photography represented a new medium for a socially committed magazine. In the period that Paul served as assistant editor he approached Devine about changing the format of the magazine, which, as Clarke Chambers has written, he considered "too stodgy, too narrow." The aims of the journal, which basically had been a vehicle to enable charities workers to maintain contact with one another, were no longer viable. With the rise of muckraking magazines more in touch with the tenor of the Progressive era, there was a need for a professional journal that would embody the values of the social welfare movement and mobilize social workers as well as those "non-professional concerned citizens."

Kellogg's suggestions apparently had immediate effect. From 1902 to 1903 *Charities* went through substantive stylistic alterations and eventually its name was changed to *Charities and the Commons*. The renaming also reflected a merger with the settlement houses associated with the *Commons* and reinforced Kellogg's belief in the necessity of editorial modifications and the character of reportage. Thus, the journal became more readable with the introduction of a new typeface, more sophisticated layouts, and illustrations as well as photos appearing with growing consistency.

One year after Hine was introduced to Paul Kellogg, he began experimenting with the display of sequential photographs and captions on a single page. This early photomontage, which is both untitled and uncredited, represents Hine's first use of a form that would later serve as the prototype for his photo stories. The story featured four photographs in varying sizes that showed children healthily at play in instructional, recreational settings— playgrounds. The piece also contained one-sentence captions. Although the photo essay does not identify the photographer, the theme (children), coupled with the signature (medium-distance shots of children happily at play), in addition to the cropped arrangement of photos are unmistakably Hine's. (Figure 7)

In relation to poverty, the prevailing belief was that people were poor not because of social or economic circumstances but due to their own laziness. Thus, photographs of people in need were at best seen as picturesque; more frequently they signified poor taste. The appearance of indigent men and women in a "gentleman's magazine" might imply that some kind of relation-

A Corner in One of the Public Playgrounds.

Chute Teeter, and Swings in the First Equipped Playground.

"Giant Stride" or "Merry-go-round."

A Typical Sand Box in One of the Nineteen Playgrounds.

F I G U R E   7

Hine's career as a serious photographer began when he and Manny went to Ellis Island. Soon after, Hine began photographing children at play. This photo essay represents one of his earliest reproduced pieces. (SWHA)

ship was called for between the reader (or viewer) and the person depicted; for a turn-of-the-century nonprofessional, no such relationship existed. Until the emergence of the "social sciences" the inclusion of such photographs in publications was seen as an invasion of privacy—not that of the people shown but of those who had to look at them.

In addition to coming up against codes of behavior, photographs of less fortunate people suffered from a lack of common, descriptive terms that might have imparted ideas of their function. The fact that, over the years, Hine had to develop his own photographic lexicon to describe his work characterizes this very problem. The terms that he both appropriated and invented included sociological photography, Human Documents, Interpretative Photography, Work Portraits, Time Exposures, and Photo Story.

This adverse relationship to photography began to ameliorate with the use of the medium in the service of social change. In 1907 Paul Kellogg was asked to direct a close-range investigation of the ranks of wage earners in the American steel district of Pittsburgh. The Survey, as it would be referred to, was apparently motivated by a request from Alice B. Montgomery, Chief Probation Officer of the Juvenile Court of Allegheny County. On June 11, 1906, she wrote to Kellogg: "Would it be possible for you to appoint a special investigator to make a study and report of social conditions in Pittsburgh? We feel that the people of Allegheny County are not as yet very wide awake as to the needs of their poor. . . ." (S.W.H.A.)

Hine, who had known the Kelloggs for two years, had just begun selling his prints and story ideas to the magazine. In light of his success, he began to view himself as a photographer as well as a teacher. Apparently, the possibility of leaving the Ethical Culture School to pursue full-time work as a photographer appealed to Hine. In 1906, two years before he actually left the School and, (probably) in response to Manny's imminent departure, he wrote to his mentor: "I have just hunted up Mr. Kellogg, Editor of *Charities*, and have started him thinking about the advisability of hiring a man (good-looking, enthusiastic, and capable, of course) to do photography for his magazine and the various societies in the building—part-time to be spent writing

for the *Charities*. As they have been in the habit of paying $2 a print, for photos they use, the economy of the effort appeals to them." (A.A.A.)

In the period prior to his joining the Pittsburgh Survey team of social workers, artists, and journalists, Hine had developed a body of work as a "human interest" photographer. He had produced pictures of child laborers in New York and Philadelphia, ventured to Ellis Island, and made photographs of street life and playgrounds in New York's immigrant ghetto, the Lower East Side.

The integral relationship of Hine's camerawork to the social welfare movement did not fully take effect until 1909 with the success of the Pittsburgh Survey issues of *Charities and the Commons*. The mutually enhancing collaborative relationship between photographer and editor would cohere in these issues. Hine, who was one of several photographers working on the team (but the only one whose photographs were credited), would have an opportunity to work with Paul Kellogg selecting, sizing, cropping, and arranging photographs for reproduction. The Pittsburgh Survey offered mutual opportunities for Hine and Kellogg to set into motion a new vision of social work and to use the journal toward this end. Kellogg wrote in *Charities and the Commons* that "The term 'survey' is a new one in social investigation. It stands for a new method; and for more than a new method." (Figure 8)

A midwesterner like Hine, Kellogg brought to the project a Turnerian-derived perspective that Chambers has characterized as an "ideal of sturdy self-reliance combined with the spirit of mutual cooperation." The Pittsburgh Survey was emblematic of an unprecedented direction in the social welfare movement, and those who worked on it were confident of its success. As the emphasis shifted from issues to individuals, pictures helped to tell the story. Kellogg's notion of orienting the Survey toward "individual health and happiness" would find structure in Hine's belief that "the individual is the big thing after all." Although the Survey represented Hine's first official free-lance assignment for the magazine, his photographs were so instrumental in the success of the enterprise that he was hired as its staff photographer in 1908.

Charities and the Commons featured three issues on the Pittsburgh investigations from 1908 to 1909. In addition to the Sur-

vey orientation, what differentiated these issues from preceding ones was the way information gathered was presented, that is, stylistic concerns. A preponderance of photographs, drawings, silhouettes, as well as maps, graphs, and charts, were used. In particular, Hine's poignant photo essay, "Immigrant Types in the Steel District," encapsulated Kellogg's dictum of showing "the great body of the working population on such an individual basis." (Figure 9) "Immigrant Types" is a multipage photo story. In many ways this essay was the cream of Hine's Pittsburgh camerawork; it underscored a tightly composed, frontal type of portraiture. (Other photographs of Hine's appeared in "Wage Earners of Pittsburgh," "The Industrial Environment of Pittsburgh's Working Women," and "The New Pittsburghers.") Hine had set a precedent in journalistic coverage of immigrants in an earlier photo story, "As They Come to Ellis Island," which was his first piece that carried the by-line "Photographs by Lewis W. Hine." This later photo story reinforced Hine's commitment to social photography and his contribution as a photojournalist.

In addition to featuring Hine's individual and group portraits, Kellogg's editing of the photographs conferred upon them the status of artwork. Certainly, Hine's formal signature resembles that of the artist Joseph Stella, whose charcoal drawings were often

F I G U R E   8

Paul Underwood Kellogg came to New York in 1901 as a young reporter and enrolled at Columbia University. There he met Edward T. Devine, editor of *Charities,* and began writing articles for the journal. Later on he was promoted to associate editor of *Charities and the Commons* and rose to prominence as director of the Pittsburgh Survey. (SWHA)

Hine's photo story "Immigrant Types in the Steel District" featured portraits of workers artistically shown in nonwork settings and was reproduced in a multipage spread in *Charities and the Commons*. (SWHA)

contiguous with his own work. Both emphasize the human qualities of the worker, who is shown in autonomous, nonwork settings—on the streets, at church, and at home. Many evidence the bustlike posture of a traditional (sculptural) portrait. (Figure 10)[10]

After the success of the Pittsburgh Survey issues, *Charities and the Commons* changed its name to *The Survey* in 1909. Paul Kellogg conceived of the new journal as a broadly educational publication operating "along the borders of research, journalism and the general welfare." Editorial policy was reformed to emphasize "first hand inquiry and investigation." The magazine's masthead was revised to show a ship "of the New World" calmly sailing through rough waters. In addition, "regular procedure involved submitting controversial articles in draft form to concerned parties, considering the suggested revisions, and checking dispirited sections and offering opportunity for rebuttal." (S.A.) (Figure 11)

In the halcyon, post-Survey issues, the editor–photographer relationship between Kellogg and Hine continued to grow. Together they further explored the potential of Progressive journalism and presented human-interest stories in novel ways. Hine wrote of "the value of the photographic appeal . . . to help the workers to realize that they themselves can use it as a lever even tho it may not be the mainspring of the works." He developed photo stories, picture essays, and Time Exposures in which the photograph became increasingly prominent. According to John Whiting, *The Survey* "broke journalistic ground" in January 1910 with a sixteen-page photo insert Hine collaborated on with Lillian Wald, Frances A. Kellor, and Mary Dreier about the state construction camps in Ashokan, New York.[11]

With a visual and political orientation established in the Pittsburgh Survey, Hine and Kellogg had created a revelatory graphic language, one centered on the common man, woman, and child. They worked as a team, collaborating on the process of editing, arranging, and combining photos with informative texts. In subsequent years *The Survey* would feature work Hine produced for the National Child Labor Committee as well as essays about tenement homework (for the Consumer's League), "street" life, and illiteracy—issues that would continue to unfold in the "story in pictures."

Drawn by Joseph Stella.

PITTSBURGH TYPES.

THE STRENGTH OF THE NEW STOCK.

The artist Joseph Stella was of Italian origin and emigrated to the United States at age nineteen. His expressive charcoal renderings first appeared in Pittsburgh issues of *Charities and the Commons*. (SWHA)

F I G U R E   11

After the success of the Pittsburgh Survey in 1909, the editors of *Charities and the Commons* changed the journal's name to *The Survey*. Three years later Kellogg was named its editor and chose as its symbol a ship drawing taken from an old map prepared by Christopher Columbus's pilot. Kellogg wrote: "We are essentially a magazine of the New World and share in its spirit." (SWHA)

CHAPTER FOUR

THE
NATIONAL
CHILD LABOR
COMMITTEE
YEARS

In 1906, while employed by the Ethical Culture School, Hine began working as a free-lance staff investigator and photographer for the National Child Labor Committee in New York City. In many ways Hine's pictures for the Committee were a natural outgrowth of his charismatic relationship to children. The National Child Labor Committee was formally organized on March 14, 1905, with Dr. Felix Adler, founder of the Ethical Culture Society, as its chairman and Owen Lovejoy its general secretary. From its inception, the Committee earnestly set out to counter the national impression that child labor was not as rampant as purported, and that, even so, its effects were not necessarily "evil." The Committee's early printed matter was without any photographic illustration.

Hine was apparently the first photographer the National Child Labor Committee hired. He promptly set precedents with direct photo reportage that presented the innate savvy of child laborers rather than showing these children in a victimized posture. Many years later Lovejoy wrote to him: "The work that you did under my direction was more responsible than any or all other efforts to bring the facts or conditions of child labor employment to public attention." (A.A.A.)

In an early speech, Dr. Adler, who had likened the movement to a "holy war," declared that "This child labor movement . . . [is] carried out in the interests of a New American civilization. . . . it is not primarily a movement dictated by pity." (L.C.) Like sister institutions seeking to improve the conditions of the poor and immigrants in the cities, such as Jane Addams's Hull House in Chicago, Lillian Wald's Henry Street [Nurse's] Settlement in New York, and Florence Kelley's National Consumer's League in New York (which fought for compatible legislation assuring better working conditions for women and children), the activities of the National Child Labor Committee were featured in the Progressive journal *Charities and the Commons*. The Committee published leaflets, newsletters, and, later, bulletins that featured national reports about child laborers. On the surface, National Child Labor Committee literature was intended to lay bare the empty future of the two million youths prematurely engaged in labor. On a deeper level, the purpose of the Committee's publications was to educate the public and stimulate popular protest in support of national legislation to abolish child labor. Prior to 1906, the printed matter was largely comprised of articles by Committee investigators who described conditions in factories, canneries, and farms across the country. On occasion these reports were illustrated with charts, maps, and statistics (the standard graphic language of social workers), but these devices depersonalized the severity of the issue for the lay reader.

As Hine began working freelance for the Committee, he envisioned himself as "an investigator with a camera." His photographs offered incontrovertible evidence that child labor existed; his captions complemented the action of each photograph. By 1907 Hine had published his first photo story, an accordion foldout leaflet entitled "Night Scenes in the City of Brotherly Love," which depicted boy messengers, newsies, and street vendors under the age of twelve selling their wares in Philadelphia. Although Hine was not credited as photographer or investigator—the author is

*T*he greatest advance in social work is to be made by the popularizing of camera work, so these records can be made by those who are in the thick of the battle.
—Lewis Hine (1909)

"The Kodak"—the signature and voice are clearly his.

Hine's photographs provided direct proof of the children's activities, but he had "to be double sure that [my] photo-data was 100% pure—no retouching or fakery of any kind," because of the public's reluctance to accept photographs as verifiable records of information.[12]

Hine developed several variations of the photo story format in his work for the National Child Labor Committee. The first is probably the simplest version and may best be described as a quasi-filmic series of sequential images typically organized into panels of picture and text. In a way, the reader views the event as if he or she were watching a film. Each successive module reveals a new element of photograph and text and literally unfolds in an ordered, linear space and time. The second leaflet Hine designed (No. 12), "The Burden Bearers," is an example of this style. Authored by "Small Kodak," it contained eight photographs and captions telling the story of child homeworkers in New York City. Unlike more sophisticated adaptations of this form, this early, unrefined photo story portrays a single event, child homeworkers delivering goods. The story itself has a feeling of closure about it despite the indeterminate sense of space in each photo. In this leaflet the captions are both in the children's voices and the moralizing tone of the photographer. They are based on actual statements the kids made to Hine or those he overheard.

The second example is more complex, although it, too, conforms to a linear arrangement of pictures and words. "Night Scenes in the City of Brotherly Love" (Leaflet No. 11) is a variation of "a day in the life" theme. The flow of the story moves from one panel to the next. It is message-oriented, and—unlike the simpler type—has a beginning, middle, and end (climax). The captions impart more of a narrative quality and include the voices of several different children in the same panel, as well as the photographer's own impressions. (Figure 12)

This early picture essay demonstrates Hine's skilled use of flashpowder. While artificial light was necessary to make these nighttime photographs, the presence of light in Hine's photographs

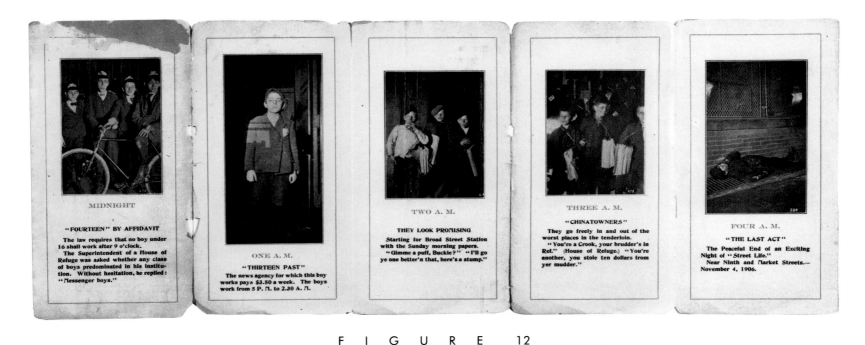

MIDNIGHT

"FOURTEEN" BY AFFIDAVIT

The law requires that no boy under 16 shall work after 9 o'clock.

The Superintendent of a House of Refuge was asked whether any class of boys predominated in his institution. Without hesitation, he replied: "Messenger boys."

ONE A. M.

"THIRTEEN PAST"

The news agency for which this boy works pays $3.50 a week. The boys work from 5 P. M. to 2.30 A. M.

TWO A. M.

THEY LOOK PROMISING

Starting for Broad Street Station with the Sunday morning papers. "Gimme a puff, Buckle?" "I'll go ye one better'n that, here's a stump."

THREE A. M.

"CHINATOWNERS"

They go freely in and out of the worst places in the tenderloin. "You're a Crook, your brudder's in Ref." (House of Refuge.) "You're another, you stole ten dollars from yer mudder."

FOUR A. M.

"THE LAST ACT"

The Peaceful End of an Exciting Night of "Street Life." Near Ninth and Market Streets.— November 4, 1906.

F I G U R E   12

"Night Scenes in the City of Brotherly Love" was the first leaflet that featured Hine's picture–text panels for the National Child Labor Committee. (NCLC)

has deeper implications. In the National Child Labor Committee lecture mentioned earlier, which was delivered in 1909, Hine elaborated on this principle. He conferred a spiritual value on light and believed that the "great social peril is darkness and ignorance." He envisioned the camera as a perfect instrument for rectifying these conditions because ". . . light is required. Light! Light in floods. . . . in this campaign for light we have for our advance agent the light writer—the photograph."

In all but one of the nine frames the children are enveloped by darkness. The burst of light illuminates them so that they emerge from the black recesses of night. In fact, the force of the flash effectively collapses the space of the frame. Foreground and background merge in a startling transformation of black space into white, negative into positive. In this flattened pictorial space, the photographer has successfully intervened to impose a tempo-

rary dispensation in the lives of these tough night-laborers.

The written portion of the story is an elaborate grouping of text, subtext, and caption. The time each photograph was made appears directly beneath it. The pictures begin at 8:00 P.M. and move successively until 4:00 A.M. The middle section of the text offers information about either the type of work the child performs or his age. The final layer provides a plot line: in a two-or-three-sentence descriptive paragraph, Hine notes the child's wages, the hours worked, the districts worked in, and how one sibling's premature labor encourages it in others. He often integrated a child's voice into this last section of text to evoke a boyish rhythm and energy.

Hine also invoked the private, intimate world of the boys by employing the language they used in speaking to one another, their vernacular expressions: "'Gimme a puff, Buckle?' 'I'll go ye one better'n, here's a stump,'" or "'You're a Crook, your brudder's in Ref.' (House of Refuge.) 'You're another, you stole ten dollars from yer mudder.'" In addition to underscoring the authenticity of his investigation, the coarse street slang effectively injects a desperate quality into their story.

By the time Hine left the Ethical Culture School in 1908, after completing the spring semester, he had successfully photographed for the Pittsburgh Survey and the National Child Labor Committee for two years. His work had appeared in Committee publications and press kits and was effective in generating popular support and recognition of the movement. The organization was pleased with Hine's efforts and hired him at a rate of one hundred dollars a month plus expenses to investigate child labor conditions throughout the country.

After several years in the liberal atmosphere of the Ethical Culture School and the privileged background of many of its students, the National Child Labor Committee represented a drastic change of scene for Hine. As Adler indicated, Committee investigators were soldiers in a holy battle. Their mission was to enlighten both the public and employers to their sinful acceptance of child labor.

While the general public may have been unwilling to seriously address the issue, management reacted to Committee efforts with increased hostility, and flatly refused agents access to their premises. As a result, inquiries were conducted systematically and under the strictest supervision. Normally, three staff members examined a workplace: an investigator, who was responsible for asking the questions and completing copious reports; a photographer, who sometimes functioned as an investigator; and a witness, who was present at the sites and, later, signed an affidavit testifying to the authenticity of both the written and visual reports. These measures not only assured complete accuracy but lent a scientific uniformity to the investigations.

During this first year in his official capacity as staff investigator, Hine alternated his responsibilities as photographer, investigator, and witness, and traveled to Indianapolis, Cincinnati, West Virginia, North Carolina, and Washington, D.C. On these early assignments Hine was congratulated for demonstrating "tact and

resourcefulness," no doubt alluding to difficulties he surmounted in dealing with recalcitrant factory managers and owners. It was also during this period that he began promoting himself as a "Social Photographer," and advertised regularly in Kellogg's journal.

The following year Hine continued his work in Chicago, where he photographed immigrants at Hull House. He also did field work for the Committee in Georgia, Connecticut, New England, and Maryland. Later that same year he traveled south to Florida and the Gulf states, and returned north via New Jersey. In addition to photographing work conditions, he prepared stereopticon slides that he employed in lectures delivered at conferences. He also began designing exhibits displayed at National Child Labor Committee expositions and assumed control of the organization and layout of his photographs and captions.

Apparently Hine's proclivities for detective work were well suited to the goals of the National Child Labor Committee. According to personal accounts of his teaching days shared with Walter Rosenblum, Hine was a first-rate actor whose antics as a "wayward tramp or itinerant peddler" delighted his students. Indeed, with growing management antagonism to the Committee's campaigns at exposing the widespread existence and exploitation of child laborers, Hine was compelled to adopt a variety of disguises to deflect his confrontations with management and enter canneries, mines, factories, farms, and sweatshops with fifty pounds of photographic equipment. One can imagine a mischievous Lewis Hine with a stack of Bibles in the crook of his left arm, a suitcase filled with photo equipment at his feet, ingenuously selling a factory foreman on the merits of owning a New Testament. While making his pitch, Hine is perhaps adjusting his tie as he casually inches his way into the factory to catch a glimpse of working conditions and estimate the number and ages of children employed. Other personas Hine adopted included postcard salesman, insurance salesman, and industrial photographer making a record of factory machinery. From the diversity of his assignments and assortment of photographs he appears to have easily mastered the skill of gaining admittance to the workplace and surreptitiously setting up shop. Using the buttons on his jacket to measure a child's height, he would cajole his subject into answering questions about the length of time he has worked, his age, name, siblings, type of work, address, daily hours, and weekly pay. If, on the other hand, all of the above guises were unsuccessful in gaining him entry, he would merely station himself and his equipment outside the workplace's entrance to photograph and interview groups of children as they entered and exited the building.

By 1910 the National Child Labor Committee was convinced of the importance of Hine's photographs in countering the idea that child laborers did not exist. He was formally hired as a full-time agent at a yearly salary of $3,000 plus expenses to continue to raise public consciousness about the issue. In 1911 his wife, Sara Rich Hine, accompanied him as a witness on forays throughout Virginia. She collaborated on reports documenting conditions in "13 cotton mills, 10 knitting mills, 5 silk mills, 3 woolen mills, and glass and shoe factories." The following year a son, Corydon, was born and the Hines purchased land at Edgars Lane in the upstate village of Hastings-on-Hudson, where they moved in 1917.

The sheer number of sites that Hine investigated is staggering, especially in a period without the benefit of air transport. The same year that Hine completed fieldwork in Virginia with his wife, his journeys took him through Missouri, Alabama, Georgia, Tennessee, Indiana, Pennsylvania, along the Gulf Coast from Florida to Louisiana, Mississippi, and up to Maine, Massachusetts, and New England. The former teacher of geography traveled over 50,000 miles in 1916 and 1917!

Hine rose up the ranks of the Committee and had succeeded Anna Louise Strong as exhibit director by 1914. While forty out of forty-eight states had laws on their books prohibiting child labor, few states policed workplaces. Thus, Hine continued to travel and produce more photographs. However, his new job added another dimension of control in the promulgation of his work.

In a sense, the exhibition medium enabled the Committee to reach greater numbers of people than the publication program. Typically, expositions offered a more sensationalistic, rhetorical message and featured sloganeering and "text as image" panels. Unlike the photo stories, the exhibits presented panels that told a story from a more generalized viewpoint: the orientation was to emphasize child labor rather than just dramatize an individual

child's plight. Hine cut out figures from his photographs and whitened or blackened backgrounds to re-use certain individuals in his collage-like panels. The new, decontextualized subject, that is, the child worker sans worksite, was then mounted onto a panel. Nevertheless, Hine appeared to have had his favorite kids, who were inadvertently used in contradictory contexts.[13]

During the time that Hine was employed by the Committee, he developed yet another combination of photos and text that he called "Time Exposures." This new visual presentation was introduced in the February 21, 1914, issue of *The Survey*, and entitled "School Opens at 6:00." From 1914 through 1915 they became his primary visual form: sixteen appeared in the journal within a twenty-month period. They emerge as some of his strongest formal statements and largely replaced the photo stories and picture essays he had developed in *The Survey* the previous decade.

In the lexicon of photography, a time exposure is one used in low-light conditions that generally lasts longer than a second. The subject must be either inanimate or capable of holding one pose for a fairly long time. The camera is normally placed on a tripod or stable surface to insure that, during this protracted interval, the camera is not jarred and the image blurred. Alternatively, a time exposure can be made indoors with the aid of a flash. In this case the camera would again be set as before, on "t" (the standard setting was "i," for "instantaneous"), but the exposure time would not be unusually long. Rather, the flash would last about 1/40 of a second and provide the necessary illumination for the film's exposure.

Examination of the photographs Hine gleaned from his personal archive of images to employ in the Time Exposures indicates that most of them were not actually time exposures—certainly not in the case of the first Time Exposures, taken outdoors. Hine's selection of this term, while not always technically appropriate, is consonant with his personal photographic vision: the creation of a new language in which to express his ideas of social reform.[14] After almost a decade as a peripatetic photographer, Hine had amassed a large body of photographs. No longer the inexperienced cameraman, after eight years he had emerged as an expert in his field.

Each of the Time Exposures is arresting in the way it communicates information about a theme readers were long familiar with, child labor. Each has its own singular form of expression, although there are certain general qualities inherent to all, such as the efficient use of magazine space (the Time Exposures appeared within the context of an article that often bore no relation to the theme Hine interpreted and occupied only a portion of the page). Also, virtually all of the Time Exposures were untitled and represented a joining of work from Hine's National Child Labor Committee archives and his artistic images of immigrants, children, and parks in New York. A unique feature of Hine's National Child Labor Committee Time Exposures is the use of extensive text, which was a departure from his standard short captions. Finally, the Time Exposures are frequently juxtaposed in diptych and triptych arrangements and occasionally offer a montagelike editing of thematically dissimilar photos into a cohesive unit,[15] although some are single images with and without photo insets.

During this same period Hine continued photographing in the streets of New York. The Time Exposures were a new vehicle where contemporaneous and old work, personal and professional work, might be rearranged and ordered—thereby extending their "time"—into lyrical statements about childhood, city life, and child labor. Perhaps the term also served as a metaphor to symbolize Hine's mature control of his subject matter, for conceptually the time exposure represents a complicity between the subject, who is actively posing before the camera, and the photographer.

Hine's Time Exposures successfully utilized language and pictures to refocus attention on child labor in a novel manner. "Three Bits of Testimony for the Consumers of Shrimp and Oysters" (February 28, 1914, Vol. 31, p. 662) emerges as one of his most sophisticated combinations of photo and text. It depicts a group of children at work in a Louisiana cannery, along with a brilliant mosaic of historical, journalistic, and investigatory text by "the Photographer," "the New York Sun," and "the Investigator." "Girl Workers in a Cotton Mill" (March 14, 1914, Vol. 31, p. 737) and "The Double Standard" (April 4, 1914, Vol. 32, p. 5) both featured single images superimposed with photographic insets along with lengthy texts. "The Industrial Revolution Up to Date" (May 9, 1914, Vol. 32,

p. 1717) contained a diptych arrangement of photographs in which a woman and child picking cotton are juxtaposed to a "cotton-picking machine that will not only save time and money, but will . . . drive women and children from the long-drawn drudgery of the fields."

Not all of Hine's Time Exposures were limited to the depiction of child laborers, however. A summertime issue of The Survey featured one that celebrated life in the city. The August 1, 1914, issue included three daytime, action photographs. (Figure 13) In the first photo, a boy flies a kite; in the second, smaller photo, a group of boys wade, fully clothed, in a fire hydrant's gushing waters; and in the third, which is the same size as the first, boys play an energetic ball game.

Despite the professional achievement that Hine's National Child Labor Committee photographs represented, and the fact that he enjoyed working with children, he confessed a personal ambivalence toward the Committee's zealous philosophy. In a letter to his former partner, mentor, and boss, Frank Manny, he confided: "I have to sit down, every so often and give myself a spiritual antiseptic. . . . Sometimes I still have grave doubts about it all. There is a need for this kind of detective work and it is a good cause, but it is not always easy to be sure that it is all necessary." (A.A.A.)

By the time Hine left for Paris in May 1918, he had produced several thousand negatives and many thousands of contact prints for the Committee. He had functioned as an investigator, special agent, witness, exhibit director, and graphics designer. He had also written articles about his experiences as an investigator, stories for and about children that included his photographs, and delivered lectures that featured lantern slides. His pictures appeared in every permutation of the picture–text marriage: photo montage, photo story, photo mosaic, picture essay, centerfold, centerfold pull-out, accordion-fold leaflet, postcard, and Time Exposures. In the twelve years that Hine was affiliated with the organization he had established himself as the nation's most prominent social photographer. Added to his cornucopia of images of the common man and woman was a sophisticated body of photos redefining the public's perception of child workers.

Time Exposures

By Hine

Little cuts like this remind us
As we flit to woodlands wild
We had better leave behind us
Playgrounds for the city child
—*G. S.*

F I G U R E   13

Each of Hine's Time Exposures was unique in its combination of photographs and text and in its modulelike appearance. (SWHA)

CHAPTER FIVE

THE PROGRESSIVES, THE PEACE MOVEMENT AND WORLD WAR I

The Great War was precipitated on June 28, 1914, in Sarajevo, Bosnia, when Archduke Franz Ferdinand, the heir apparent to the Austro-Hungarian throne, was assassinated by a Serbian youth protesting the loss of his country's independence. As war engulfed all of Europe, American social activists, political leaders, and journalists who had successfully worked as a group to effect reform in American society saw their community begin to disintegrate. Although the Progressives had been unified in activating domestic economic and social reforms, they were of conflicting opinions as to what role the United States should play in the new international crisis. The Progressive Movement was splitting into two camps: those who believed it was America's obligation to "save humanity," and those who did not favor expanding the social welfare movement internationally.

Thus, the war years emerge as a time of tumultuous upheaval and change for the Progressive coalition. To protest the war, prominent leaders of the New York social community, such as Florence Kelley, Owen Lovejoy, Edward Devine, Paul Kellogg, and Lillian Wald, met on September 29, 1914, and established the Henry Street Peace Committee. Their initial reluctance to address the social issues of war and peace was gradually replaced by a growing recognition that demand for overseas relief funds threatened to curtail domestic programs. Paul Kellogg ultimately emerged as spokesman for the group and attributed the members' unwillingness to officially take a stand to the fact that, unlike their work in the social sciences, they could not wholeheartedly approach the problem of internationalism with the "first hand knowledge"

The entry of the United States into the war has profoundly affected every reach of American social life and every social relationship. . . . It has demanded that all function in new ways. . . . The social movement will be needed not merely as a mender and patcher and critic of things, but as an affirmative force, and the Survey *can be one of the channels through which it expresses itself.*
—Paul Kellogg

earlier employed in earnestly dealing with Progressive issues.

From 1905 to 1914, parallel to the growing popular support for domestic reforms during the muckraking era, a Peace Movement had been created. It began among local religious groups as an attempt to abolish the "evil" of war. Then, feminist reformers, cultural leaders, and big businessmen formed societies, committees, and foundations to implement the goal of international peace. After almost a decade of peace awareness and a feeling that, as Merle Curti has expressed it, the "dawn of international peace could not be far off," war hysteria gripped Europe, and the Peace Movement in the United States crumbled. At this early stage of war, American newspapers began to reflect a renewed interest in the heroic and patriotic promise of war. While editorials did not specifically endorse sending soldiers overseas to fight alongside the Allies against German aggression, in the wake of war fever an American "Preparedness Movement" was created. (Figure 14)

At this same time, a small group of Progressives emerged as outspoken pacifists in an attempt to mitigate the rising tide of pro-war emotionalism. Jane Addams, for example, a prominent social welfare leader in Chicago, was a visionary who understood the profound connection between international peace and the advancement of social welfare programs. Rallying against William James's popular argument, set forth in *The Moral Equivalent of War*, that militarism satisfied man's need for "obedience to command and martial virtues," she proposed that the same energy be used to abolish poverty and disease. Inspired by a burgeoning sense of the soli-

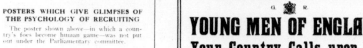

F I G U R E   14

Kellogg's pacifist position was reflected in this spread, "which gives glimpses into the psychology of recruiting." (SWHA)

darity of an international Women's Movement, in December 1914, Addams, along with Charlotte Perkins Gilman and the European feminist Rosika Schwimmer, launched a Women's Peace Party in Washington, D.C.

With Addams's international campaign to promote peace, the Progressive community reevaluated its anti-internationalist agenda. Subsequently, nearly all of the members of the Henry Street Peace Committee revised their strategy to manifest support of military efforts overseas. According to the historian C. Roland Marchand, Edward Devine, Paul Kellogg's former boss and a member of The Survey's editorial committee, wrote about the important function social workers served in the "organizing and training [of a] nation for war." Lillian Wald was involved in war mobilization and Florence Kelley served as secretary to the Board of Control of Labor Standards for Army Clothing. Despite the change of heart evidenced by these members of the Progressive community, a handful of their stalwart colleagues were unwilling to support wartime activities.

For Lewis Hine the wartime years were a period of heightened artistic activity. It was during this time that Hine produced his Time Exposures and first called the combination of pictures and text a photo story. Although he had been affiliated with Progressive programs for more than ten years, and had publicly lectured in support of child labor legislation, his political views were usually articulated from a professional, i.e., work-related, standpoint.[16] In relation to the first World War and the social issues pertaining to war and peace, it is Hine's reproduced photographs that characterize his pacifist position.

Within two months after war swept through Europe, Hine created a photomontage for The Survey entitled "The Girls They Leave Behind Them," which encapsulated his neutral position vis-à-vis internationalist concerns. Because Hine's piece also reflected Kellogg's dismay with the public's growing interest in the war, the montage emerges as an editorial. The text in the center of the spread ironically comments on the interconnectedness of nations: "It is estimated that the industrial army of America contains one million reservists subject to call in various European armies." (Figure 15) Hine appropriated the compositional prototype, Madonna and Child, and selected six photographs of immigrant women and their infants from his library of Ellis Island photographs.

Nearly one-and-a-half years into the war, The Survey reproduced one of Hine's photographs on its January 29, 1916, cover that depicts two young boys happily engaged in a mock duel; the boys are fighting one another with wooden sticks. The picture was apparently made prior to 1914, probably during the period when Hine was photographing children at play on the Lower East Side. By using a photograph of children "at war" he is able to symbolically address man's internecine habits. In the text he interprets the folly of war by noting how the popular press manipulated public opinion to generate war fever: "WAR TIME. . . . Here as abroad the spirit of adventure, the fight instinct and the glamor of soldierly display and combat overpoweringly appeal to the excited youthful imagination through picture and story in the daily papers. . . ."[17]

During the first two years of the war, President Woodrow Wilson, a scholar and early supporter of the Peace Movement, championed American neutrality. Nevertheless, with inflammatory articles in the press on Bulgaria's ruthless genocide of Serbian civilians, and Germany's sinking of the Lusitania, many Americans vociferously railed against Germany and began to take sides. Wilson, who was reelected in 1916 on the campaign slogan "He kept us out of war," had begun to be swayed by the warnings of the Preparedness Movement. By January 1917, when Germany reinstituted unrestricted submarine warfare, the prospect of the United States' entering the fray had gripped the country. Even members of the Peace Movement restructured their thinking to endorse Wilson's new rhetoric; they saw America's entry into the European War as a way "to end war" and to "make the world safe for democracy."

With ample newspaper coverage of exciting wartime events such as military parades, in which smiling soldiers march past flag-waving crowds, popular sentiment grew to be more and more against neutrality. At this same time, 1915 to 1916, many more social workers began to view the Peace Movement internationally, as a logical extension of the various social welfare measures each had personally struggled to make possible.

The girls they
leave behind them

It is estimated that the
industrial army of
America contains one
million reservists subject
to call in various Euro-
pean armies.

Photographs by Hine

F I G U R E   15

Hine was essentially allied with *The Survey*'s editorial staff in their opposition to the war in Europe. His position was evident in statements in which the interdependent relationship of photographs and text was explored. In this instance, Hine specially designed a photomontage featuring immigrant women and their babies along with a politicized inscription. (SWHA)

By 1917, while the nation was increasingly absorbed in the process of mobilizing for war, Kellogg had published a peace issue of *The Survey* in which he called for a national referendum on American involvement in the war. Yet, for those who had been overseas and witnessed the carnage, another attitude was prevalent. Eliot Wadsworth, acting chief of the American Red Cross, responded to his editorial on February 17, 1917: "The policy which you lead up to in your process of reasoning and advocate for the United States does not appeal to me as a practical one in the present crisis." In April of that year, the United States entered the war, and the Progressive coalition was once again polarized into two groups: internationalists who supported involvement and desired to help in the postwar construction of a democratized and reformed new order, and liberal pacifists, such as Kellogg, who opposed militarism and the war itself, but intended "to hold on to" those national reforms and programs he had fought to implement.

By mid-1917, however, Kellogg's attitude began to change. Support for his ideas dwindled when several of his colleagues successively left for Europe to work in war relief programs. Edward Devine traveled to France to become director of the American Red Cross refugee mission in Paris; Homer Folks, another member of the Progressive community, arrived in Paris in July to direct the American Red Cross's Department of Civil Affairs; and Graham Taylor, who had been in Russia since 1916, was attached to the American Embassy at Petrograd and did relief work among interned Austrians and Germans. As New York's community of social reformers became more directly involved in relief programs overseas, and a flow of information between *The Survey*'s offices and Europe was made possible, Kellogg was compelled to modify his position with respect to war-related issues. Soon after, he followed in his colleagues' footsteps to personally report on the American Red Cross's special programs overseas for *The Survey* and was converted to internationalism.

Kellogg arrived in Paris in September 1917 to write a series of articles on reconstruction work in France and Belgium. He initially functioned as an inspector for the American Red Cross and worked under the direction of Major Grayson M.P. Murphy, United

States Commissioner to Europe. Later on he was enlisted by Homer Folks to join his Paris staff as acting chief of the editorial bureau, Department of Civil Affairs. Encouraged by what he saw, Kellogg extended his trip by several months. After reporting on relief work in France, Belgium, and Italy he returned to New York in early 1918.

How Hine came to work for the American Red Cross is not especially clear. Apparently, in a discussion between Kellogg and Homer Folks, his name was mentioned as another possible recruit for European relief work. Upon returning to New York, Kellogg encouraged Hine to join Folk's team in France and subsequently wrote to Folks of his interest. On May 22, 1918, directly after Hine had terminated his ties with the National Child Labor Committee, he was officially hired by the American Red Cross as Folks's special assistant and photographer. Later that week he journeyed to Paris, the Red Cross's base of operations. After more than a decade of traveling from virtually one end of the United States to the other, Hine had his first and only opportunity to photograph northern and southeastern Europe.

CHAPTER SIX

CENSORSHIP OF THE PRESS AND ITS EFFECT ON THE AMERICAN RED CROSS

In his startling examination of war photography, Jorge Lewinski has characterized news coverage of the first World War as "the greatest conspiracy to delude the public about the effects of war." Referred to as the Great War, or European War, World War I was marked by twice as many casualties—9,000,000 soldiers—as there had been in all the major wars of the previous 125 years combined. (Figure 16) The war's iniquity lay in the development of trench and chemical warfare that deformed and maimed countless soldiers. With the increasing horror of the war, the Allies established an unyielding system of press control, only releasing approved photographs through military censors and in government-sanctioned military reports. In addition, patriotic and inspirational scenes were staged, such as mock battles, to be photographed for propaganda purposes.

At the outset, however, the press was permitted access to areas where the fighting was most intense, but to make photographs a special permit was required. To assure a consistent representation of the war, photographers usually had the added benefit of a military escort who advised them about the kinds of pictures that portrayed the war properly.

*T*he coming of peace will release masses on masses of intensely, vitally interesting pictures of the achievements of our soldiers and airmen which censorship has heretofore prevented our publishing; consequently the Mid-Week Pictorial will be able to present a far more graphic picture-history of the war than at any time since it began publication.
—New York Times Mid-Week Pictorial Editorial of November 21, 1918

during the first World War are imbued with incredulity as he described the professional difficulties photographers encountered throughout Europe. His postwar articles in *Leslie's Illustrated Weekly* reported that a photographer "risked death" in England if he was found making photographs of civilian wartime activities, such as parades and recruitment campaigns, without government authorization. And England was not atypical in its special requirements for the press. In a biography of Hare by Lewis Gould and Richard Greffe, the authors recounted that in France, after "an associate had warned him . . . that all reporters and photographers are to be rounded up and arrested tomorrow . . ." he "found England more hospitable and caught the first boat back."

Until 1917 the war was a European conflict, only real to the American public insofar as it was written about and depicted in newspapers and magazines. As the war continued, the public's appetite for pictorial coverage increased and descriptive accounts appeared regularly in the daily press. In addition to military-sanctioned reports that provided one view of the war, the American press was dependent on reports and photographs distributed through a new government agency, the Com-

Despite wartime censorship, photographers continued to be sent overseas by the popular press. Jimmy Hare was an English combat photographer whose work was featured on the pages of the American pictorial journal *Collier's Weekly*. He was probably the most famous war photographer of the late-nineteenth and early-twentieth centuries and proudly proclaimed that he "never faked a picture." Hare's candid observations about censorship

mittee on Public Information, which President Wilson created one week after war was declared. George Creel, chairman of the Committee, was a former journalist and a liberal. His job was both to disseminate select facts about the war and to coordinate government propaganda efforts. Creel described the Committee's activities in his book, *How We Advertised America*, as "a plain publicity proposition, a vast enterprise in salesmanship, the

F I G U R E   16
The Flanders region of France and
Belgium was among the most
devastated areas on the Western
Front. (CAH)

world's greatest adventure in advertising."

A group of photographs that Hine produced during the war reflected the type of pro-military publicity the Committee endorsed. Apparently commissioned to do so by the vernacular publication *Everybody's Magazine*, just after the United States entered the war, Hine made hundreds of photographs of the Army and Navy camps, particularly those of the "Rainbow" (multi-ethnic) division stationed in New York City. Three of his photo stories were featured in *Everybody's* in July, September, and October of 1918, while he was in Europe. The corny titles of the stories, "Playtime at the Training Camp, The Soldier's Life is Not All Work," "The Stuff that Makes Our Fighting Force," and "The Yankee Stew—A Bit Too Hot for the Kaiser," aptly described the pictures reproduced.

Like the two spreads that followed it, "Playtime" is a two-page photo story that presents a series of giggly soldiers engaged in an assortment of daily activities that seem to have been especially enacted for the photographer. The young men shave, wrestle, frisk a cat, and entertain visitors in a parody of martial self-control and stoicism. (Figure 17) Although Hine apparently was not directly involved in the editing and cropping of the pictures, the layout does have some design panache: its top line features oval shaped photos, partial cut-outs, and full-frame pictures in alternating sequences. The bottom two rows present four photographs of the same size, arranged in a measured sequence of two pictures to a page. The captions reflect the silliness of the photographs, "Boudoir secrets," "Wounded in the funny-bone," "Grooved," "Wrastling is popular," etc. As with all photographs that related to wartime activities, the Committee's stamp of approval is affixed to the verso of several of the original prints.[18]

A group of three images showing the reconstruction of a

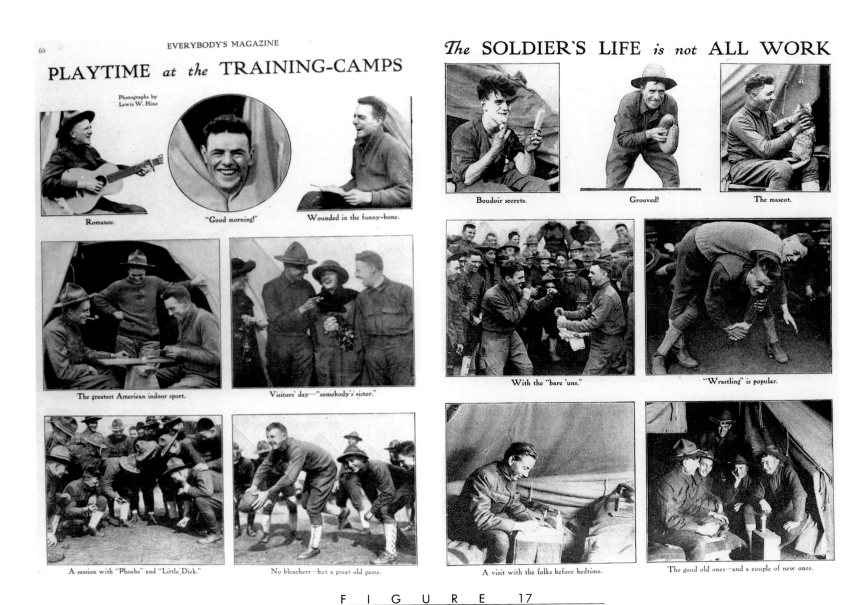

FIGURE 17

In 1918, prior to Hine's departure for Europe, *Everybody's Magazine* apparently commissioned him to produce dozens of photographs featuring young soldiers and sailors. The journal reproduced a selection of these pictures in three essays. (SWHA)

Before and after. It was not until 1937 that one of these
photographs was reproduced, for pictures of mutilation were not
published during or just after World War I. (LC)

French soldier's face—not made by Hine—illustrates why the au-
thorities suppressed pictures. In the first photograph the young
poilu confronts the camera in a portraitlike pose, his military med-
als proudly displayed. Even though a wan smile appears on his
lips, the picture is painfully effective—the soldier's eyes have been
gouged out. In the second photograph an American sculptor,
Mrs. Anna Coleman Ladd, and her assistant are making a mask
of the *mutilé*'s face in a process designed by a British captain
named Derwent Wood. (Figure 18a) Working with old photographs
of the soldier's "normal" face, they make a mask out of thinly
rolled copper, which is silvered over and painted in a flesh tone.
The piece was held in place with bows hooked over the ears.

This technique was used widely both during and after the
war as a way of aiding the thousands of soldiers whose faces had
been grotesquely deformed, but this is a particularly poignant
case. In the last photograph of the series the soldier is attended
to by the assistant, who is adjusting his eyeglasses. While the
mask and eyeglasses give the appearance of a healthy man, in
fact, neither has restored his sight. (Figure 18b)[19]

One organization that benefited greatly from the activities
of the Committee on Public Information was the American Red
Cross, particularly after 1916. Not only did the Committee mobilize
popular support for Red Cross fund-raising drives, but it also
arranged for corporations to donate huge sums to its overseas
relief programs. In wartime promotional campaigns, the Committee choreographed a total of $100 million for the Red Cross and
related government-approved relief organizations in Europe.

With the advent of the first World War the American Red

Cross had gone through a period of unprecedented growth and change. It "accomplished on both sides of the trench line a work which could not be advertised in wartime." (S.W.H.A.) Arthur Schlesinger has explained that in addition to providing medical relief to injured soldiers, the Red Cross "safeguarded the interests of soldiers' families at home, took charge of sanitary conditions in the civil districts or adjoining camps, distributed comfort articles among the soldiers, aided refugees outside the war zone, recruited ambulance companies, and trained and directed nurses."

Like the popular press, the American Red Cross was dependent on official photographers and national press liaisons for coverage of its own war-related activities. It published *The Red Cross Bulletin*, *The Red Cross Courier*, and *The Red Cross Magazine*, which were essentially promotional and fund-raising vehicles. With press restrictions increasingly rigid and the press's distorted picture of the war masking the plight of Europe's masses, by 1916 the American public became less interested in supporting war-relief efforts. The growing numbers of military casualties and civilian refugees in Europe put the American Red Cross in desperate need of funds to maintain its work. At the time it appeared as if the entire relief network would collapse due to lack of support. Arthur Kellogg wrote to Paul, who was working for the Red Cross in Europe, that there was also a feeling within the organization that the agency was "in danger of failing to interpret itself to the public. . . . Mr. Norton said . . . absolute necessity for every man who holds an important position in the R.C. to go to France. . . . such an expedition . . . was all that was necessary to make a man the most ardent advocate of the work now going on in France and Belgium." (S.W.H.A.)

Although President Wilson attempted to maintain a position of neutrality, he was under increasing pressure from corporate and political interests to send American troops overseas. In addition, the public was increasingly aware of German brutalities, which were especially publicized by former *Collier's Weekly* editor Arthur Gleason to motivate American participation in the war. Gleason, an associate of Kellogg's, had enlisted in the Belgian army as a stretcher-bearer from 1914 to 1915. He was captured by the Germans and brought back the first accurate accounts of

German atrocities, which were published in the *New York Tribune*.[20]

The crisis that beset the American Red Cross alarmed government officials, who read it as a sign of U.S. weakness. To mollify this sentiment, Wilson moved closer to the Preparedness Movement. One of his first actions was to create a War Council within the American Red Cross, which included Henry P. Davison, Charles Norton, Grayson M.P. Murphy, Edward N. Hurley, and Cornelius N. Bliss, Jr. He usurped the powers of its (then) virtually all-female administration, and substituted businessmen who would gain money, prestige, and power from American participation in the war.

Still, the agency experienced administrative problems that hampered the efficacy of its activities. In a letter to Paul Kellogg, Homer Folks wrote that there was "a failure of the Red Cross to send over an adequate staff of inspectors and agents for the Bureau of Refugees." (Homer Folks Papers) While Peace Movement activities had all but ended as Americans became more enraged by reports of German aggression, the Red Cross screened all prospective employees and censured those who had participated in peace-related programs. A wartime memo reads in part: "The Bureau of Personnel has apparently been very nervous in the matter of people who have had any connection with peace activities in the pre-war stage." (S.W.H.A.)

Once the War Council was in operation, the agency was treated like a military arm of the Federal government. Uniforms, as well as military ranks, were given to all Red Cross executives. And, for a period of time, its photographers, journalists, and administrators were permitted access to areas ordinarily restricted to the press. Like any social-service organization, the Red Cross required the aid of photographers whose pictures could convince the public of the importance of its overseas work, particularly in civilian relief. Lewis Hine was one of thirty-seven photographers hired by the agency to work in Europe. His human-interest photographs may represent the largest, semi-unrestricted body of work done by an American Red Cross staff member of postwar reconstruction. In the tradition of the picture–text strategy, his photographs would be employed in post-Armistice photo stories in *The Survey* to generate support for reconstruction programs and the new agenda of internationalism.

CHAPTER SEVEN

LEWIS HINE
IN
EUROPE

By the time the United States entered the first World War in April 1917, Hine had been promoting the activities of the National Child Labor Committee for twelve years. His photo stories and photographs had appeared regularly in national magazines and were a staple in *The Survey*. Despite the Committee's success at alerting the public to the inherent problems of child workers, it had not managed to effect the passage of a Federal child labor law. The hope of enacting such legislation was diminished once American troops were sent overseas. At this point the country's priorities shifted from domestic programs and reform to a growing recognition of the central role the United States would play in world politics.

In the spring of 1918 Hine approached the National Child Labor Committee for a salary increase. Instead, the Committee voted to reduce his salary from $275 to $200 a month. Because he had been seeking new sources of income, Hine had either anticipated its decision or had already decided to join members of the Progressive community in European relief work. By June 1918 Hine had arrived in Paris. In many ways Hine's work for the National Child Labor Committee prepared him for the grueling ordeal of his European tour. In the period Hine worked for the Committee, he had traveled extensively by train, car, and foot. His varied investigative techniques had also given him a solid background for photographing in difficult and unfamiliar situations.

The Red Cross job, being a wartime assignment, represented a unique situation for Hine as a photojournalist. It involved traveling to a continent engulfed in conflict and photographing the human angle of the war. In the final analysis it was one of Hine's most prolific and creative periods. During his eleven-month tour he produced approximately 1,500 negatives: from early June to mid-November 1918 he made approximately 500 negatives of Paris and its environs, and from late November through April 1919 he produced about 1,000 negatives in France, Italy, Serbia, Greece, and Belgium.

In later years Hine looked back at his European photographs as a transition between his early documentary work and later celebrations of the industrial worker. He later explained his motives in the October 1938 issue of *Survey Graphic*: "In Paris, after the Armistice, I thought I had done my share of *negative* documentation. I wanted to do something *positive*." After years of laboring to educate the public about the social, economic, and political discrimination experienced by immigrants, the poor, and child laborers, his postwar pictures were in support of rather than in opposition to society's larger goals—the reconstruction appeal in Europe and the entry of the United States into world politics. Hine's photographs further explored his celebration of the common person and traversed lines of ethnicity and gender. Indeed, the European stories are more expansive in their comprehensive depiction of the diversity and quality of life abroad. They show civilians—men, women, and children—and soldiers of many different nationalities, all of whom are engaged in a struggle to reconstitute their lives.

The sequence of events leading to Hine's employment by the American Red Cross is a bit obscure. His New York associates Edward Devine and Florence Kelley had been involved with Euro-

The American people will be given an opportunity, such as has not been given before, to visualize how much must be done in order to rehabilitate the lands over which the Germans have waged brutal warfare.
—Paul Kellogg

pean relief work for two years, and his colleague Paul Kellogg had spent several months in Europe as *The Survey*'s war correspondent from 1916 to 1917. Homer Folks, the former secretary fo the State Charities Aid Association, was a major in the American Red Cross and director of the Department of Civil Affairs in France. After Kellogg returned from Italy, Folks hired him to work in the Publicity Office of the Department of Civil Affairs. Subsequently, Folks worked closely with Kellogg and apparently mentioned that he was looking for an assistant and photographer. Perhaps Kellogg had recommended Hine, knowing of his growing dissatisfaction with the National Child Labor Committee. Nevertheless, it appears as if the Kelloggs acted as "go-betweens" because by March of that year Hine had written a note to Arthur that said: "I guess the France job fizzled out." Two months later Hine joined the Ameri-

can Red Cross Commission to France at a salary of three hundred dollars a month. (Figure 19)

Since the American Red Cross fell under the jurisdiction of the American armed forces, Hine essentially entered the service at age forty-four, well over draft age. Like all American Red Cross executives, he was given a temporary rank of captain and fitted out with a para-military uniform replete with officer's hat and high boots, which facilitated access to restricted military areas. Unlike some of his colleagues, such as Folks, he did not elect to bring his family overseas and was separated from his wife and six-year-old son for nearly a year.

Major Folks, a tall, distinguished, mustachioed man, was seven years older than Hine and a prominent New York sociologist identified with the antituberculosis campaign and public health work. After completing his courses at Albion College in Michigan he obtained a degree at Harvard and subsequently came to work in New York. While Hine and Folks had a mutual respect for one another, their backgrounds as professionals created two distinct approaches to social work. Obviously, Hine's photographic background stressed both a visual and humanistic orientation to social work that was underscored by the success of the Pittsburgh Survey. Folks's background had been structured by a "charities" sensibility common in the 1890s. He was, for example, a staunch proponent of eugenics and the social gospel. Despite differences in their backgrounds, Folks recognized the value of Hine's unique vision.

In Europe, Folks pursued his work with a characteristic seriousness and earnest intensity. He had been in Paris since the summer of 1917 with his wife and two daughters, and was responsible for organizing and directing the Department of Civil Affairs and its bureaus dealing with tuberculosis, child welfare, cripples, relief in war zones, and aid for refugees. The department also implemented reconstruction programs in devastated areas throughout France. On August 27, 1918, Folks became director of the Department of General Relief, a job that led to his appointment as director of the Special Survey Mission on November 11, 1918.

At the outset, Hine and Folks worked separately. While Folks administered the department, Hine photographed its activities and related Red Cross programs. Other than a summer assignment to photograph the Child Welfare Exhibit at St. Etienne, Hine apparently had no specific daily responsibilities and was not supervised in his work. However, one of Folks's intentions in hiring Hine was to collaborate with him on a writer–photographer basis. Folks, for example, had already written twenty-four short articles on various phases of Red Cross relief and reconstruction work, but these pieces usually did not utilize photographs.

Hine's first months in Europe were spent in Paris and environs, chronicling the activities of the Bureau of Refugees and Relief, Bureau of *Mutilés*, and Children's Bureau. These initial photographs have been the most problematic to isolate. Since many photographers had been hired to photograph Red Cross activities for fund-raising purposes, most of the pictures are somewhat nonde-

script and the photographer is not usually credited. As a rule, they show Red Cross personnel cheerfully administering to the sick, injured, or orphaned. There are many photographs of nurses in action, such as those dressing soldier's wounds, attending to their hospital rounds, or assisting doctors' examinations.

Folks's Department of Civil Affairs had organized a Child Welfare Exhibit in the summer of 1918 that turned out to be Hine's first formal assignment. He photographed demonstrations in the Children's Hospital at St. Etienne on how to bathe your child properly and examine him or her for signs of illness or malnutrition. The exhibit also provided material on proper diet.

The St. Etienne photographs have a didactic, illustrative quality unusual for Hine's European work, but one that would be seen with growing frequency throughout the 1920s and 1930s. Most of the photographs were made indoors under conditions that necessitated both the use of a tripod and artificial light. The contact prints are 5x7 inches, and few have captions. A typical pho-

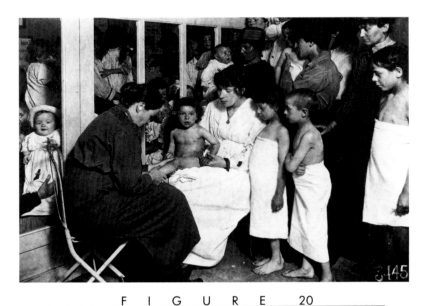

F I G U R E 20

Folks's decision to mount child hygiene demonstrations at the Children's Hospital was inspired by "The Babies Saving Show," an exhibition in Lyon where he delivered an address. (GEH)

tograph of this period is Figure 20, which bears the inscription: "Dr. Bonness and her assistant explaining child hygiene to mothers at the American Red Cross Child Welfare Exhibition at St. Etienne, France, 1918." All of the children are wearing large white towels wrapped around their legs and middles. The youngsters and their fully dressed mothers gaze dutifully at Dr. Bonness while the subject—an infant girl propped up on an examination table—stares wide-eyed at the cameraman.

In another picture Hine showed relief workers in action. This photograph, made under less formal conditions, pictures a group of four young children resting in bed, with three of their little friends standing at bedside. The children are attended to by a Red Cross nurse. On a Red Cross poster above their heads, an ageless woman shelters a wounded soldier in her arms and exemplifies the tire-

less efforts of American Red Cross personnel at protecting the helpless and sick. For these young orphans this *pieta* also represents the essence of the organization as "the Greatest Mother in the World." (Figure 21)

In addition to privileges as a Red Cross executive, Hine apparently had a unique relationship with the agency regarding ownership of his prints and negatives. In July 1918, he sent a number of his earliest photographs at St. Etienne to Paul Kellogg for possible reproduction in *The Survey*. Today, of course, it would be unusual for a photojournalist working for one agency to approach a newspaper or magazine independently and try to sell a photo story. In this case it is clear that Folks was interested in having the work of his department publicized in Progressive magazines like *The Survey*. Hine wrote: "At Major Folks suggestion, I have put

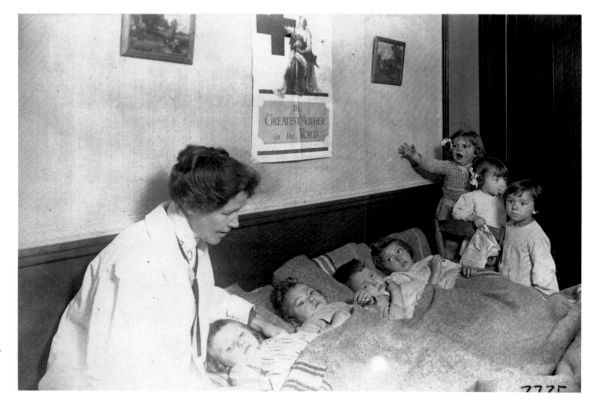

F I G U R E   21
The St. Etienne photographs represent Hine's first wartime photo assignment for the American Red Cross. (GEH)

together a bunch of my recent photos at St. Etienne which I think might lend themselves to a photo spread for the Survey. If so, give me a credit line as staff photographer A.R.C. in France. If not, would you kindly send it down to the Art Dept. of *Everybodys* magazine?" (S.W.H.A.)

On other forays Hine produced candid "street" photographs. A group he made in a railroad station delicately reveals the emotional turmoil caused by the war. One photograph shows two elderly women and a man, each with lost, somewhat benumbed expressions on their faces, sitting with a grandchild. With several bags piled at their feet, they await a train that will take them out of Paris. In Hine's coverage of activities at the Red Cross relief station he also photographed a young orphan girl, her arms possessively wrapped around her lone vestige of home, her dog, and another little girl enjoying a bowl of soup. These humanistic war photographs predate by twenty years pictures associated with a school of photojournalism that has been known by the name "concerned photographers."

Hine's photographs of the city show torn war posters pasted to the sides of empty, aging buildings, deserted Parisian streets, and refugees on queues outside relief stations. Millions had left the cities for the safety of small villages and farms—only 10,000 people were living in Paris in the spring of 1918. Of the thirty-four photographs in the International Museum of Photography at George Eastman House made at the beginning of his tour, many graphically show the immeasurable emotional torment the French endured. As visual information they were made for an American public unaware of the extent of human suffering throughout Europe. As potential fund-raising instruments for the Red Cross, they emerge as some of Hine's most affecting photographs.

Despite the grim realities of wartime France, Hine's fascination with Europe was made wonderfully clear in his attempt at recreating—and indeed discovering—a special, "pre-wartime" Paris and France. These photographs reveal an uplifting, personal side of Hine's work that contrasts with the frightening, war-related images. In the summer and fall of 1918, Hine toured areas of northern France, including Normandy and Le Havre, as well as cities west and south of Paris such as Tours, Bordeaux, and Toulouse. From the inscriptions on the verso of existing prints it appears that these were the first photographs he made for himself rather than the agency. Interspersed with Red Cross shots of orphans, the homeless, and injured and mutilated soldiers, the photographs have a refreshing, lyrical quality that is simply inspired.

In an unprecedented departure from his usual fast-paced, one-or-two-exposure work method, Hine made eight separate pictures of a woman he called "Joan of Arc" of Tours. The photographs portray a dark-haired, mysterious-looking young woman with her eyes gleaming upward. He captioned one of the portraits, "After Chapu—Listening to the Voices." And while several different positions of "Jeanned'Arc" [sic] were shot, they did not have the rhythm, organization, and action necessary for a photo story. Rather, they seem to represent a gesture on Hine's part to connect with a spiritual presence, one created to ameliorate the cruel and inhuman destruction of Europe that he witnessed.

Intermittently, during the summer and fall of 1918, Hine continued to produce a portfolio of images that are redolent of an essential Frenchness in the same way that his child labor and immigrant portraits are infused with America's Progressive spirit. A photograph of an elderly woman of Bordeaux sitting within her newsstand, her dog standing calmly beside her, offered a vestige of French life as it was before the war. It also characterized a mood of optimism and survival, as does the picture of a delivery boy in Chateauveaux, or Marie Montbusion washing her laundry on the banks of the Seine, or the family working on their barge named "Jesus," or the gypsy in Montmartre talking to his parrot. Other photographs presage his work on the reconstruction survey in the Balkans, and in northern France and Belgium. These interpreted changes that war had wrought, such as the picture of a woman looking toward an empty horizon that reads, "Been waiting in this hut for four years for son to return. Havre."

Thus, the wartime portraits emerge as a distinct and special group of artistic photographs within the photojournalistic orientation of Hine's European work. Viewed independently they emanate rich, celebratory, and enduring aesthetic qualities. Certainly the preponderance of French children point to Hine's picturesque intentions, as do the titles of the photographs themselves, "Good Morning Normandy," "Child at Fountain," etc. Yet these same spontaneous street scenes, when contextualized and seen as the preface to the emotionally wrenching Balkan and Reconstruction Survey photographs, may be construed as but a temporary dispensation from the wretched effects of war on human life.

At some point during his leisurely tour of France, Hine apparently had an opportunity to photograph at the front. A single photograph entitled "Soldier in trench—smile (Letter from Home)" recalls Hine's superficial style, in which young soldiers are gleefully, if unconsciously, immersed in every possible extramilitary activity. In this picture a merry soldier reads a letter. Although the young man is in uniform, his head protected by a steel helmet, there is no genuine sense of danger or that he is even on a battlefield. Rather, the photograph follows in the tradition of the *Everybody's* spread—straightforward, frontal, and frivolous.

Hine was one of dozens of photographers hired by the American Red Cross to document its relief activities, but many more photographers affiliated with newspapers and magazines were also covering the war. However, censorship and military restrictions severely affected the dissemination of pictorial and textual information about the war. Whereas Hine had certain military advantages not available to civilian magazine photographers like Jimmy Hare or Paul Thompson, his photographs were oriented for Red Cross publications. They featured a humanistic side of the war, and favored individuals over groups when possible. Along those lines, Hine set out to photograph American doughboys recuperating at the American Red Cross hospital in the summer of 1918. *The Red Cross Magazine* featured these pictures, in photo story format, in a four-page spread. (Figure 22)

At first glance *The Red Cross Magazine* story has the same

Our All-American Army

Photographs by Lewis W. Hine of our soldiers at a Red Cross
Hospital in Paris showing the many nationalities within our army

A REAL AMERICAN—OF FRENCH PARENTS

"OI'M OIRISH, CAN YE GUESS IT?"
In a census of nationalities at a Red Cross Hospital near Paris, soldiers
of Irish descent were twice as numerous as those of any other nationality

FROM TRAGIC ARMENIA
This Armenian citizen of America has overwhelming reasons for fighting the Germans

100 PER CENT AMERICAN
An Indian turned in a few generations
into a defender of his America

"ARE WE DOWNHEARTED?"
It takes more than a wound to dim Giussepe's or Tony's or Angelo's
smile. The sunshine of Italy is reflected in their happy faces

F I G U R E   22
Although Hine was hired by the American Red Cross, the
organization used very few of his photographs. "Our
All-American Army" appeared in *The Red Cross Magazine*
in February 1919 and was a continuation of Hine's interest in
"showing the many nationalities within our army." (ARC)

silly, self-conscious outlook as Hine's photo stories for *Everybody's*. Yet, the captions in this later spread more clearly express Hine's earlier intentions in making photographs for *Everybody's*: he sought to demonstrate the ethnic diversity of the armed forces. Entitled "Our All-American Army," the essay recalls a style reminiscent of studio portraiture. Hine presented group and individual medium-distance shots of an Armenian, German, Italian, Scot, Jew, Viking, Greek, and Pole. Some of the men strike a formal pose for Hine; others face the camera with joyous spontaneity. There is, however, a casual quality to the photos reinforced by the fact that each soldier is in his hospital pajamas and bathrobe. The captions impart a decidedly patriotic feeling, but one characterized by youthful spirit.

The photographs' stylistic consistency, however, is counterposed by the variation in captions. One is in a colloquial, humorous voice: "Oi'm Oirish, Can Ye Guess It?" while the Viking forthrightly adds, "I fight for Norway, too. The Germans have been sinking our vessels and killing our men." In a bit of scientific reportage, Hine included a line that confirmed the Army's ethnic make-up: "In a census of nationalities at a Red Cross Hospital near Paris, soldiers of Irish descent were twice as numerous as those of any other nationality." Hine's article featured individuals—good old American working-class, heroic guys who were fighting to make the world safe for democracy. Although Americans struggled to redefine their relationship to "foreigners," that is, Italian-Americans, German-Americans, Jewish-Americans, etc., Hine's work posited the bravery of the individual immigrant.

In October 1918 the Red Cross announced the formation of a special commission to document the needs of refugees throughout Europe. A publicity release reads in part: "At the request of the War Council for the Commission of Europe, a comparative picture of actual needs existing in European countries is to be prepared. The countries to be visited are France, Italy, Servia, Greece, Palestine, Switzerland, Belgium, England, possibly Russia, Roumania and other Balkan states." (Homer Folks Papers)

Folks, who had been promoted to lieutenant colonel in anticipation of his new responsibilities, received a letter from H.D. Gibson, chairman of the American Red Cross Commission to Europe on October 24, 1918, which outlined the goals of the survey:

> . . . In each case the picture of the necessities is vividly painted, and that there is tremendous need we have not the slightest doubt. In view of the fact, however, that the work is unlimited, it is necessary for us to have a scientifically studied picture of the comparative necessities of the various countries in the lines of work which we have been engaged. As to how this picture should be prepared and the analysis made, details will be left to you. . . . The order in which this trip is to be taken will be left to you and your judgment. (Homer Folks Papers)

Folks responded eagerly to the challenge and wrote back that same day: "I am hoping that my mission may not only help the American Red Cross to make its appropriations, but that I may be able to put together an accurate statement of civilian conditions in Europe resulting from the war." Within three weeks, Folks would select a team of men to accompany him on this campaign. While all these preparations were made prior to the Armistice, by the time the Special Survey team was ready to start out, the war had ended.

As Folks's wartime assistant and photographer, Hine would have an opportunity to accompany him and explore other regions of Europe. In many ways his photographs represented a new iconography for the American Red Cross. Rather than focusing on the Red Cross itself as a sign of the agency's beneficence or its personnel in action, Hine pictured the civilians who had been helped by the Red Cross. In this respect, and particularly in relation to war-connected issues, he dignified the victims of war. Thus, his photographs function as a nonrhetorical effort at increasing support for Red Cross programs.

"Portrait of woman." (GEH)

"Paris—gamin—fishing Seine bank." (GEH)

"Good morning Normandy." (GEH)

"Itinerant worker resting at the entrance to
a large chateau near Paris." (GEH)

"Old woman with umbrella." (GEH)

"He hops the taxis with agility. Paris."
(GEH)

"Norman Fisher boy at Omstreham."

"Eiffel Le Grand Driving Cows Home."

"Neuf Chattlan Gamin . . . Occasionally."

"Barge Maiden, (France) Toulouse."

"Bordeaux paper woman." (GEH)

"Two peasant women at market." (GEH)

"Listening to voices. A native Jeanned' Arc
[sic]. Tours, France. After Chapu." (GEH)

"Toulouse—seventy-three years old." (GEH)

"Been waiting in this hut for four years for
son to return. Le Havre." (GEH)

"Delivery boy (France) Chateauveaux."
(GEH)

"Paris—delivering laundry." (GEH)

"Child with doll." (GEH)

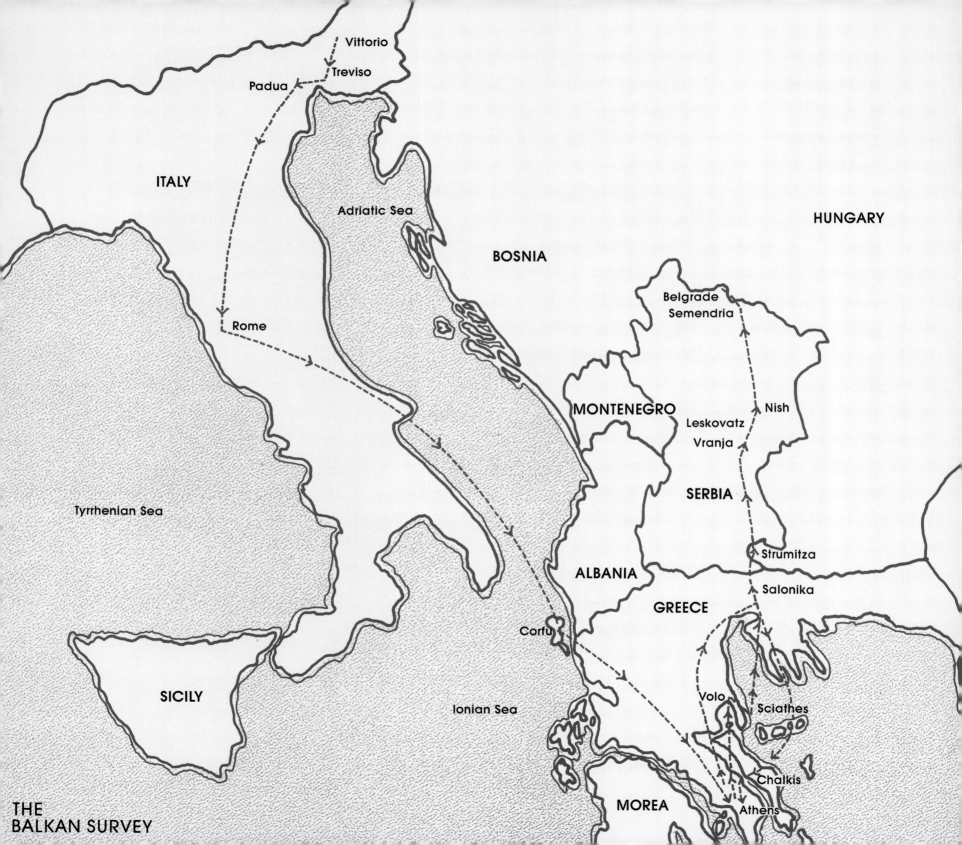

ITALY

Vittorio

Treviso

Padua

Adriatic Sea

BOSNIA

HUNGARY

Rome

Belgrade
Semendria

MONTENEGRO

Nish

Leskovatz

Vranja

SERBIA

Tyrrhenian Sea

Strumitza

ALBANIA

Salonika

GREECE

Corfu

SICILY

Ionian Sea

Volo

Sciathes

Chalkis

Athens

MOREA

THE
BALKAN SURVEY

Despite a working relationship with local American Red Cross chapters, its Paris executives apparently were not well informed about the extent of devastation throughout Europe. Unaware of the lack of adequate transportation and the state of the roads, Folks originally planned to travel as far north as England and as far east as Rumania within a ten-week period. However, he wrote to George F. Canfield, president of the State Charities Aid Association, on October 24, 1918, "I doubt if there is any possibility of getting to Russia. . . ." (Figure 23) In a letter to Paul Kellogg, written on the day of his departure three weeks later, Folks indicated that his schedule was only slightly revised, and added, "I expect to blow into New York about February first."

Folks was keenly aware of the professional opportunity the Special Survey represented. As special commissioner to southeastern Europe and a senior American Red Cross executive, he would be the first person to survey, administer, and write about conditions of postwar peace. As a transplanted New York social worker, he also viewed his work within a revised Progressive program, one that coupled internationalism with domestic reform. He had successfully adapted the social welfare prototype, such as he had administered in the State Charities Aid Association in New York, to the special needs of France. Now that a truce had been declared, he set out, as he explained in his book, *The Human Costs of the War*, "on a unique mission . . . to find out at the end of a great war how much suffering there was, and of what kinds."

The Special Survey Mission was scheduled to depart on November 11, 1918, which coincidentally proved to be the same day the Armistice was declared. That evening, Folks left Paris for Italy and the Balkans. Because of the confusion in the streets created by the Armistice celebrations, only four of the six team members accompanied Folks to Italy: Captains Edward S. Godfrey, M.D., epidemiologist; Lawrence Pumpelly, interpreter; Lucien W. Booth, secretary and stenographer; and Lewis W. Hine, photographer. Captains Edwin G. Miller, food administrator, and Louis I. Dublin, a tuberculosis expert, met the team in Italy a day later. The journey was not only to survey the destruction in Italy and the Balkans but to distribute food and medical supplies. The team traveled by boat, train, automobile, and foot. (Figure 24)

F I G U R E   24

The American Red Cross Special Survey team. Folks is pictured at the far left and Hine at the far right. (GEH)

Hine's gymnastics as a photographer included this daring feat in Paris. (GEH)

priorities that later provided an outline for his book. These included transportation, food, clothing, medical needs, and public health. In his photographic work Hine developed his own list. The Balkan Survey photographs seem best arranged in thematic groupings: street scenes, modes of transportation (the migration homeward), child laborers, and subcellar and outdoor dwellings. On his first tour, Hine made only a handful of photographs of American Red Cross workers directly engaged in servicing civilian needs. His photographs addressed the greater implications of Red Cross work, that is, the social and human issues relating to postwar reconstruction and rehabilitation.

On one level the pictures that Hine produced in Europe may be viewed as a reflection of themes he dedicated himself to in his American work. But conditions in Europe necessitated a different approach and a new interpretation of familiar subjects. And, although some of the subject headings may be similar, Hine's European work represented a revision of style. Often working quickly, he abandoned the formal constraints imposed by the tripod to make images with a new purpose, that of showing the devastation of the countries and people he saw juxtaposed to relief activities of the Red Cross. Yet, there is a subtlety to this connection, since the Red Cross presence is often an implicit one.

Hine's lifelong commitment was to what he called "social photography." His aim was to represent his subjects in the most complete, least "artful" way possible. With minimal intervention of "style," he wanted his audience to feel all the conflict, tension, and beauty inherent in the experience of his subjects. Hine believed that a photograph was "a symbol that brings one immediately into close touch with reality." This approach to photography reached its fullest expression in Hine's coverage of war and peace, which provided a more visceral context for his aesthetic.

While the operation of Hine's "European" camera was the same as his "American" one, Hine made several of the Balkan images at an accelerated shutter speed. For most of Hine's photographs, the 4x5 Graflex was hand-held with its shutter speed set at 1/125th of a second. A factor that determined a variant shutter speed was whether or not a subject—or Hine himself—was moving and in what relation to the picture plane. And, in terms of

Aware of the importance of their work for American Red Cross fund-raising efforts, Folks organized a list of categories or

depth of field, the camera's 135mm lens generally gave Hine more latitude than the longer-lensed 5x7 Graflex.

One major drawback to the Graflex was that it did not have a "swing back." To change from a horizontal to a vertical format he had to unscrew the back of the camera and manipulate it into a different position. In his early National Child Labor Committee work, Hine appears to have settled on a format and worked consistently with the camera in that position. In his World War I pictures, horizontal and vertical photographs are interspersed. Usually, when he wished to make a close-up of a child he would work in vertical format and then crop the print.

In the European photographs Hine's formal signature, his use of a posed, frontal, medium-distance shot, is augmented to encompass a candid, more expansive, point of view. His photographs have a freer, more modern look appropriate to the photo story format. For Hine, the proliferation of photographs in newspapers, books, exhibits, and lantern slide presentations was proof that photography was "the language of all nationalities and all ages." For Folks, this was no doubt a consideration in hiring a photographer to accompany the team.

In Europe his interest in conflict reached new forms of expression. Like the photographs he earlier produced for social agencies, the Italian and Balkan images were to be employed for promotional purposes. A year after the Armistice, they would be released to show the public the need for its support to remedy desperate conditions overseas. Yet, the images of Europe were made with an awareness of the "limitless" need of the population; in that way they differed from the didactic work Hine frequently produced for the National Child Labor Committee.

In a departure from the posed shots prevalent in his pre-European work, Hine's signature now depicted action shots from skewed and aerial vantage points. He crouches to make portraits of children in Greece, stands atop fences to produce candid images of refugees converging on Red Cross relief stations, and photographs the devastated landscape of northern Europe from a moving vehicle. In Paris, he employed the support of two doughboys, each of whom held on to a leg while he stood atop a balustrade to photograph the city from dizzying heights. Hine's

FIGURE 26
The new role of the U.S. (ARC)

photographs have a dynamic look one associates today with photojournalism. As Folks lyrically wrote, "By his remarkable photos of various types of persons seen on our travels he helps us to understand that these people are of the same kind as ourselves, and to realize, not only that we are our brothers' keepers, but that our brothers are well worth keeping." (Figure 25)

Both Hine and Folks kept notes about the people they met, the conditions the team surveyed, and the general situation in each village or city. Ordinarily, Hine's notes were reproduced as captions with his pictures. In the European work, Hine's text was incorporated into the captions appearing on the verso of the American Red Cross prints, but his words were not always used when the pictures were reproduced. In *The Survey*, for example,

SEPTEMBER 6, 1919
PRICE 25 CENTS

RECONSTRUCTION
NUMBER FOR SEPTEMBER

THE SURVEY

THE LONG DAY—*Photo by Hine.* [See page 813]

Food Conditions in Germany After Peace Was Signed
By Jane Addams and Alice Hamilton

Uncle Sam: Jailer
By Winthrop D. Lane

A Reconstruction Health Program
By John R. Commons

F I G U R E 27
A reconstruction issue. (SWHA)

Hine made the photographs and apparently worked with Kellogg on the layout, but Folks wrote most of the text.

In relation to his reproduced pictures, the negatives that Hine produced were treated as raw material to be manipulated and cropped to accommodate a magazine's format and the syntax of the essay. For example, most of the Italian and Balkan photographs in the collections of the Library of Congress and the Commission on Archives and History have been cropped along their perimeters. However, while Hine's child labor photographs were sometimes cut up and recombined in assemblages for poster exhibitions, his European photographs were employed in "straight" reproductions in Folks's book and in the photo stories. In fact, Hine collaborated on three of the photo stories with Folks. They ap-

peared in 1919 reconstruction issues of *The Survey* and bear the inscription, "A Photo Story by Lewis W. Hine and Homer Folks, Special Survey Mission of the American Red Cross." A fourth piece was an article by Folks, excerpted from his (forthcoming) book, and an independent two-page photo story of Hine's.

The Survey prided itself on being the only publication besides the American *Red Cross Magazine* that featured special reconstruction issues. (Figure 26) Paul Kellogg wrote to his brother: "*The Survey*, like the RC, the YMCA, The Recreation Commission, should measure up to its opportunity. In the next ten years international relations will crystallize for centuries. *The Survey* can follow and interpret the social factors." (S.W.H.A.) In both an effort to support and interpret Red Cross postwar relief campaigns and to address the revised role of the social welfare movement in international politics, Kellogg produced several reconstruction issues. Hine's spreads were featured in all of them. (Figure 27)

In these stories Hine selected a specific group of photographs that may not individually read as his strongest pictures, but they reinforce each other as a unit. A number of his photographs were enlarged to heighten the action of the story, but they were not bordered, silhouetted, or fragmented in quasi-cubistic configurations as was sometimes the case in National Child Labor Committee literature, particularly in its centerfolds. The point of the European essays was to simply and forcefully present a panorama of the scope of human desolation ameliorated by American Red Cross relief workers.

When Hine first employed the term "photo story" in 1914 his primary interest was to use current photographs to describe the saga of child labor. There was a uniformity to his National Child Labor Committee photo stories, one might even say a sameness, for the photos were usually of equal size and essentially conveyed a theme from a single point of view. This was remedied by his creation of the Time Exposures. However, a successful photo story uses a group of photographs in varying sizes (usually the work of a single photographer) to tell a story from several points of view.

While not all of the postwar photo stories manifest a sophisticated use of the format, two of them do. In these the arrangement of photographs is kinetic and imparts a strong visual continuity.

A Greek shiner on his native heath (Athens)

GREECE passed a child labor law in 1912. In October, 1917, all labor laws were suspended on account of the war. Of the stonebreakers, below, the youngest (apparently ten and twelve years of age) said they were fifteen and sixteen, and were paid thirty cents a day

A tiny news-girl on the streets of Belgrade

...ty asserts itself over the burlap sack filled with shoes, bread and decayed fruit, picked up along the wharves of Salonika

Repairing the country roads of Greece

Tenement home-work in Athens

A juvenile butcher in (Athens) street market

Two young coppersmiths (Athens)

F I G U R E   28

"The Child's Burden in the Balkans" (continued on page 110) in *The Survey* was the last collaborative photo story Folks and Hine worked on. It represented a departure from the standard gridlike arrangement of Hine's prewar photo stories. (SWHA)

A MACEDONIAN
GUNGA DIN

"*THE uniform 'e wore
W'as nothin' much before,
An' rather less than arf o' that
behind;
For a piece of twisty rag,
An' a goatskin water-bag
Was all the field equipment 'e
could find."*
— KIPLING.

*MOTHERS and children, picking out
nut meats in these filthy cellar ruins
of Saloniki, recall the shocking child labor
scenes pictured by Mr. Hine for the National Child Labor Committee in New York
city tenements in 1911.*

*THESE Serbian girls, driving their
oxen, are living and working in
a wonderfully picturesque setting,
viewed objectively. But for the child
beautiful scenery affords little inspiration when long hours, bad weather,
poor food and an almost entire lack
of schooling dwarf both intelligence
and imagination. [See the Underfed
Nursling in the Atlantic for August.]*

This came about through alternating the sizes and shapes of pictures in relation to each other. The progression of the narrative is also conveyed through a kind of cinematic manipulation of the pictures, or editing. The first picture may "establish" the story line through a close-up. The next photo may introduce an even broader viewpoint. The success of, for example, "The Child's Bur-den in the Balkans" depends on the relationship between the photographs; as one moves from one picture to the other a whole story emerges.[21]

An example of a well-executed photo story is "Kids is Kids." Here the presentation of photographs is "open," a departure from the standard gridlike arrangement. One aspect of this photo story is its emphasis on detail, often conveyed through a human-interest close-up or photograph cropped into a close-up. The photos in this presentation also impart a more elliptical sense of time and place, having been produced over a period of several months and in several different countries. "Kids is Kids" represents a more evolved photo story, one that provides in-depth coverage and the "feeling" of an event through different children's points of view.

Of course, any successful photo story is also dependent on text, but the role of the text is to complement the photographs. It is in regard to text that Folks's and Hine's voices resonate with the generational differences discussed earlier. In contrast to Hine's use of specific information in his captions, Folks arranged his material in such a way as to depersonalize and objectify conditions throughout Europe. His reports are filled with numbers that indicate percentages of malnourished people or statistics about infant mortality. In his book, the section under "health conditions," for example, includes a body of information on "infant welfare." It advises: "compare number of births each year during the war. . . . also death rate under one year of age. . . . what preventive measures could be taken quickly. . . ." In the section marked "war orphans" he suggests to "number the war orphans. . . . special provisions if any, made for them. . . . existing special needs for care. . . ."

In the diary that he kept throughout the tour, which later served as his notes for subsequent collaborative photo stories and his book, Folks recounted daily appointments with American Red Cross and civic leaders, relief needs in particular towns, anecdotes, and problems the group endured traveling. A reading of Folks's journal gives an overall impression of an unctuous paternalist at work. For example, refugees are typically nameless and readily ascribed to categories like "single mother," "orphaned child," and "crippled man," and they live in "unsanitary" or "picturesque" conditions. Of course, the emphasis on generic data as well as facts, figures, and statistics was necessary in some ways so that relief work could be effectively implemented. But it often reinforced an authoritative distance between Folks and the people he served that is evident in his writings.[22] (Nevertheless, Folks's achievements at directing relief programs were officially acknowl-

edged by the French Government when it named him a Chevalier of the Legion of Honor on May 26, 1919.)

While the writer–photographer collaboration should have represented an ideal use of each man's special skills, as we shall see, their photo stories were not always successful. With regard to *The Human Costs of the War*, the captions were often abridged or an amalgam of both of their voices. Ordinarily, Hine provided the pictures and captions. With the European photographs, however, Folks rewrote many of Hine's captions only to have them modified and edited for publication or reverted back to Hine's original text. In Folks's captions descriptive terms like "primitive" frequently appear, and the language is generally loaded with judgmental albeit positive assessments like "the Serbians are a hardy race." While this re-editing is not unusual, what emerges is that Hine's original text (and pictorial impressions) at times varied from Folks's homily-like remarks.

Perhaps the best example of their differences in voice is revealed by researching the alterations in a caption reproduced in Folks's book *The Human Costs of the War*. For publication purposes, the captions seem to have been edited at least three times. The original captions, which were typed onto the photos' verso, were Hine's. While preparing his manuscript Folks apparently decided to take some liberties with Hine's captions and rewrote them. By comparing the textual information Folks used for the first draft of his book, which was entitled *In the Wake of the War*, we can learn a great deal more about what these differences in perception and sensibility were.[23]

In a good example, the text beneath the photograph facing the title page reads: "The Night Before Christmas. Serbian refugees in the stable of an old Turkish inn at Lescowatz, Serbia." In Folks's typewritten notes or original version the caption reads: "A family of refugees driven out of eastern Macedonia by the Bulgars have found refuge in a stable near Leskovatz. Truly life has reverted to its most primitive form here." In an unposed photograph of this same scene, Hine's caption reads: "Greek refugees huddle together in an old building at Lescowatz, Serbia. They had been driven out of Macedonia (Seres and Dana) into Serbia, near Nish, by the Bulgars. They were on their way home when this photographer called on them. The building was in a deplorable state of repair."[24]

In another instance, the caption on page 55 for the photograph at the top reads: "Plowing in Serbia. Agriculture in Serbia, if not modern, is not primitive. The scrawny cows evidently resented the double job of giving milk and plowing ground." In Folks's original manuscript the caption read: "Primitive Plowing. Since all the men went to war, women have had to do all the hard work of the farm. An ox and cow hitched together pull the plow. The lack of draught animals has forced this peasant to use a dairy cow for plowing."

While the collaborations represented work the two men did after the survey had been completed, during the actual campaigns Hine was frequently on his own. After years of meeting the rigid expectations of National Child Labor Committee assignments, Hine operated under a freer, more subjective and journalistic aesthetic in Europe. Rather than conforming to a specific outline of survey goals, Hine set out to "discover" people who symbolized his vision of Europe after the war. It is to Folks's credit that he encouraged his "assistant" to follow his own instincts.

The first stop on their itinerary was Italy. After an overnight train ride, the Special Survey team landed in Turin on November 12, 1918, and a day later left for Rome, Padua, and Treviso. As the group was traveling by train into Italy, Hine photographed several groups of Italian soldiers, "returning prisoners of war." The prisoners had journeyed from Austria, with wrapped (bandaged) feet and tattered uniforms, using the railroad tracks as their guide. Throughout their tour of Italy the survey team would meet young soldiers in "twos and threes, in scores and in hundreds." In a sense these blurry, candid pictures, often taken from a moving train window, emerged as a metaphor for all of Europe returning home—refugees, prisoners of war, and soldiers.

In the five days that the team spent in Italy, members surveyed sixteen cities and villages. In many ways the photographs of Italy are a mild, misleading introduction to the rigors of relief work. Later on, Folks evoked his experiences in Italy in his book: "Here and there family groups of refugees were returning, the children, in spite of all their hardships, looking as irresistible as

only Italian children can look. They were cold, hungry, and homeless, but they were incomparable."

Obviously, Hine was as taken with Italian children as Folks and photographed them with great eagerness. Taking full advantage of his "street" aesthetic, he set out along the byways and thoroughfares of towns to photograph the joyous celebration of daily life that is synonymous with Italian culture. He photographed a young operetta star using a wooden crate as her stage. When a camion stopped to unload clothes sent by the city of Como to destitute people in Oderze, Hine made a humorous photograph of the town mayor, a rooster of a man, strutting about.[25]

The intimacy of these moments was facilitated by Hine's working method. Once the team entered a village or city, Hine worked by himself. Without his tripod and flashpowder "t" bar, he was free to wander wherever he wished. A lot of what he saw, however, was not always celebratory. He entered a hospital to make a poignant image of Giuseppe Ugesti, he chronicled villages such as Conegliano where he found "large numbers of women and old people in line [for food]," and meandered around tiny streets where he photographed women washing fruit and vegetables at a town square spigot. On rare occasions Hine applied a "directorial mode" and posed his subjects. He made two photographs, for example, of the tubercular Ugesti, one in which he is wearing a white woolen hat and one without.

Like France, Italy had suffered horribly during the war. The land in the area stretching from the Piave River west and north was a desolate region. In addition to the loss of thousands of men in battle, countless civilians had died from lack of food, water, and medical supplies. And, there was an unusually high proportion of fatherless children. Nevertheless, in looking at the photographs of Italy, one has the sense that Hine did not opt for "negative" documentation. Instead, he tried to show the beauty of the Italians and how their life sustained its own vital rhythm.

From Italy the group boarded the *Odessa* for the Greek island of Corfu, where it landed on November 23. Folks wrote: "Our transportation experiences from here on may well be narrated in some detail, for they reflect better than anything else the complete breakdown of the movement, both of persons and goods. . . ." When the team arrived in Athens, after endless car problems, Folks learned "that we were in a country in which the entire population had at one time been in sight of starvation."

The survey team spent about two weeks in Greece, during which time Hine made many photographs of squatters and child laborers. In these particular pictures the connections between his American and European work emerge. In both he pursued the task of depicting the plight of those in exile and premature workers. The photographs of Bulgarian and Turkish squatters in Salonika, Greece, living in abandoned factories, city streets, small caves, and bombed synagogues evoke the same empathy as his portraits of immigrants on the Lower East Side. However, the less rigid style of the first World War photographs gives them an added pathos.

However, in his pictures of child laborers throughout Greece (and Serbia), several factors converge to complicate issues involving their presentation: first, unlike the tone of his investigative photographs for the National Child Labor Committee, in Europe Hine opted for a more "upbeat" depiction of life in the Balkans. Thus, the children have a looser, more appealing look than their counterparts in his American portraits and are often smiling or giggling in the picture. Second, the collaborative photo stories that Hine and Folks worked on reflect their mutual concern for the problems presented by child labor but do so in confusing ways: while Folks's text continued to impose a critical, analytical attitude toward child workers, Hine's pictures countered this perspective. It is almost as if Hine was unaware that the European photographs depicted his subjects as being gratified by their work.

While the transfixed posture of the children in Hine's early American photographs is a sign of their miserable condition, in his European pictures the children are shown happily at work. Yet, the captions—which appear to be in Folks's voice—note the injustices of child labor in Greece and Serbia. Hine's photographs contradict this statement: the children not only appear to enjoy being photographed but seem quite content with their work.

Perhaps it was the dire poverty that Hine and Folks witnessed that etched a final picture, one at odds with Hine's own photos, in their minds. "A Macedonian Gunga Din" is part of a larger photo story entitled "The Child's Burden in the Balkans," which was an attempt to render child laborers in Serbia and in Greece. (Figure 28) At the top of the page is a poem by Rudyard Kipling that reads in part:

> . . . For a piece of twisty rag,
> An' a goatskin water-bag
> Was all the field equipment he could find.

The poem reflects the poverty the team saw in Athens and Salonika, a city that Folks portrayed in his book as "dirty, without any sort of qualification; it smells to heaven. . . . In Saloniki, old men, barefooted, dressed in pieces of burlap packing—it is mid-December— are beasts of burden."

Nevertheless, nearly all of the children in Greece are pictured doing constructive labor. The four photographs in this story picture a young water boy angling to balance his cup while he fills it with water, a proud Greek shepherdess who faces the camera with the haughtiness of a starlet, a mother and children picking out nutmeats, and a young Greek girl with her oxen. Note Folks's text, which among other things inaccurately identifies the two girls as Serbian: "These Serbian girls, driving their oxen, are living and working in a wonderfully picturesque setting, viewed objectively. But for the child beautiful scenery affords little inspiration when long hours, bad weather, poor food and an almost entire lack of schooling dwarf both intelligence and imagination." While the Special Survey team's focusing on this issue from an American perspective is understandable, the post-Victorian rhetoric of the State Charities Aid Association—and the National Child Labor Committee—is inappropriately applied.

A didactic, Committee language unmindful of Greece's postwar economy surfaces again in the second part of the essay: "Greece passed a child labor law in 1912. In October 1917, all labor laws were suspended on account of the war. Of the stonebreakers, below, the youngest (apparently ten and twelve years of age) said they were fifteen and sixteen, and were paid thirty cents a day." (See page 109) Just as the stonebreakers cheerfully face the camera in the midst of their work, so does a young girl performing "tenement home-work in Athens," a "juvenile butcher in (Athens) street market," "a Greek shiner on his native heath," and "two young coppersmiths." Unlike conditions in the United States, where child labor was a form of enforced slavery, in eastern Europe it often represented an opportunity or apprenticeship. Conditions in wartime Europe meant that jobs requiring skill—stoneworking, butchering, coppersmithing—were suddenly available. In wartime Greece, work was not only necessary but represented a chance to acquire a skill at a young age. Indeed, happy children typically symbolized the nonworking "normal" child in America. In eastern Europe, postwar cultural definitions involving work had changed to accommodate the reality that a labor force in the millions had been lost. Thus, superimposing an American strategy onto Greek and Serbian children muddled the issue. Nevertheless, Folks and Hine would have other opportunities in which to cite the hardships invoked by child labor.

With the sixth and seventh photographs the spread takes another direction. A tiny photograph of "a tiny news-girl on the streets of Belgrade" shows a ragged child, barely dressed for winter, selling newspapers. The large photograph to the right shows another young girl carrying a "burlap sack filled with shoes, bread and dried fruit, picked up from the wharves of Salonika." The pained expressions on these two girls' faces are in sharp contrast to the other children pictured, who are happily engaged in work. In effect, the photo spread is an ambiguous exercise: it primarily shows children constructively working, only to contradict this theme with a photograph of a distressed child trying to sell newspapers (the smallest in the spread) juxtaposed to a photo of a child who has been reduced to scavenging (the largest in the spread). Again, the photographs and text counterpoint one another, but the pictures do manage to convey the need for American financial support.

From Salonika the team hoped to journey overland to Belgrade where no Americans had been during the war due to the dire state of its transportation system. Folks wrote that there was "no railway service, no horses and the roads were barely passable." Thus, the team was advised to avoid making trips into the interior, but Folks balked at this suggestion and claimed that their mission was not "to simply arrive at Belgrade. Our object in coming was to see the interior of Serbia first hand." He went on to say

F I G U R E 29

In this atypical photograph, American Red Cross workers are shown distributing clothes to Serbian orphans. (CAH)

that the team was "looking forward . . . to Serbia, the country whose heroic defense in the early days of the war had won the surprised admiration of the world."

To facilitate their journey the team took on an additional member, Captain Radimir S. Chepenitch, first secretary of the Serbian Legation, who expedited official arrangements and translated. Folks's diary entry conveys some of the discomforts in Serbia: "December 17, 1918, left Saloniki at 11:45 for Uskub (Skoplie) by special train, made up partly of military cars and partly of Grecian Serbian hospital cars. No heat or light . . . weather very cold toward morning. Dressed with all the clothes I could keep on, and with the blanket and blanket-roll covering, was just warm enough." Thereafter, the team spent the better part of the trip in a military truck provided for their personal transport.

Serbia's defense of her national borders cost the country

dearly. Physically, it had been devastated as badly as Belgium—which was thought to have been the country most damaged. The effect on the civilian population was an unusually high suicide rate among Serbian women. In addition, there were no children under three years of age. (The suicide rate rose steadily until December 1919, one year after the Armistice had been declared.) (Figure 29)

As guests of the Serbian government, the team was housed in hotels or amongst privileged families in town. Folks was often confined to his hotel office, but he obviously enjoyed accompanying Hine on his exploits. A journal entry describes one morning when he "assisted" Hine in Lescovatz: ". . . went with him to take pictures of Greek refugees from Macedonia. . . . Then went to take photos of Albanian refugees camping outside a hospital." In a letter to his wife he added: "I don't think Hine was ever so happy in life as here. Something new every minute that he wants to snap. He is out all day picking up interesting things on every hand." (Homer Folks Papers) (See also footnote no. 24.)

Indeed, Hine's street photographs in Serbia are filled with wonderful discoveries. In one, a young boy dressed in an oversized, cast-off military uniform poses with his violin. Although his face is disfigured by a skin disease, the child's mournful eyes emanate a deep beauty. The scale of the instrument accentuates his youth, for it is nearly as long as his extended arm. Yet, the violin is raised to his neck in a gesture of great eloquence!

In another, a blind fiddler sits against a wall, with a crippled man to his left and two women to his right. The dynamic movement of the wind catches the skirt of the standing woman, billowing it out and unfolding it in an almost visceral momentum. The eye concedes to the rhythm of the fabric and follows the edge of her dancing skirt into the group.

In a third, a young Turkish child turned away from the camera smiles shyly into the distance. Well dressed and contented, the child is otherwise unremarkable except for the elaborately patterned clothes he wears. However, in an unexpected textual counterpoint, the caption of the photograph reads: "No—this Turkish boy is not a girl. He wears these braids in memory of his two sisters who died." Because of the singular forcefulness of this photo-

graph (and text) it was not used in any of the photo stories.

While these individual photographs represent Hine's unique perspective on eastern European life, the photo stories were an attempt at a shared vision between him and Folks. The first photo story on which they collaborated was "The Pull of the Home Tie," which appeared in *The Survey* on July 5, 1919. (Figure 30) In a series of five pages, photographs of varying sizes depict how people returned home—by foot, wagon, boat, and train. The lengthy captions below the photographs, some of which occupy more space than the pictures themselves, describe the story in vivid detail.

This multipage photo story set a precedent for the two other stories that followed it, "They Departed into Their Own Country," and "The Child's Burden in the Balkans." While the arrangement and number of photographs and text differed in every spread, each had a first page that featured an enlarged Hine photograph and several paragraphs of introductory text. Invariably the cover page gave equal space to picture and text and credited Hine and Folks.

In "The Pull of the Home Tie," the first page reproduces a photograph of a caravan of fully loaded oxen winding their way around a mountain road. Beneath it are three paragraphs authored by Folks. The action of the picture is arranged on a diagonal; one caravan has just entered the frame at its bottom right while the first fades into the horizon line. It is a striking photograph and, from its organization, one senses the slowness of the oxen's pace and the migration homeward.

The diagonal motif is continued on the second page of the story where four photographs show other modes of transportation. One is subtitled "Burden Bearers" and shows a family of four children and their father walking home through Serbia to Albania. The photograph on the facing page is subtitled "The Serbian Express" and is frontally composed. It portrays a large Serbian family seated in a boxcar waiting for the train to resume its journey. Yet, the family in the boxcar was at no advantage. The caption, which was taken verbatim from the verso of Hine's American Red Cross print, is in his voice: "This box car, standing on the switch at Strumitza just across the boundary from Greece in Serbia, was

BURDEN-BEARERS

THESE refugees setting out from northern Siberia were headed toward Albania. Serbia's main railway, the dark line in the background, was out of commission. There was no other means of communication, so this family had to walk several hundred miles. Their few earthly possessions were in the packs on their backs. Every member of the family down to the five-year-old was a beast of burden, stooping under his load as he trudged along the muddy highway over which during the past few years invading armies had marched and retreated, as other armies had done from time immemorial.

THE SERBIAN "EXPRESS"

THIS box car, standing on the switch at Strumitza just across the boundary from Greece in Serbia, was housing three refugee families returning to their former homes near the Allied line. Two children had died en route. They had been living in the car for five days. The survey party was traveling by "express." Even the express stopped for three hours at this point. When asked how far they had come the man said, "Two days by horse and cart or three by train!"

GROUP of refugees on the good ship Pelopponesus, a Grecian coastwise boat. They were going from Volo, one of the most malaria-infested towns in the world, to Kavalla in eastern or Grecian Macedonia, the part of the territory surrendered by King Constantine to the Bulgars and devastated by them.

GREEK priest at Leskowatz, Serbia, helping a group of refugees back to their homes in Greece. The British Tommies were giving them a lift in their lorries. They were from Greek Macedonia, near Seres, sent by Bulgarians into northern Serbia, and now were more than half way back.

F I G U R E 30

"The Pull of the Home Tie" appears in *The Survey*. In this picture essay we can see the prototype for magazines like *Life* that followed almost twenty years later. (SWHA)

housing three refugee families returning to their former home near the Allied line. Two children died en route. They had been living in the car for five days. The survey party was traveling by 'express.' Even the express stopped for three hours at this point." When asked

THIS is a refugee village established by the Greek government for Greeks from eastern Rumelia, where they had lived for many centuries until it became part of Bulgaria in 1908. The Bulgars wanted them to give up their churches, schools, language and nationality. So they set out for Greece, expecting the storm to blow over and meaning to go back "home." The people among whom they settled did well by them and they are prospering. Nevertheless, they have no idea whatever of remaining here permanently. All plan to go back. They have been here for ten years but feel confident that some change in the shifting boundaries of the Balkans will permit them to go home to eastern Rumelia and still be Greeks in language and nationality. Great is the force of nationality but greater still is that original and most powerful of all the factors in conservatism, the love of the home soil.

LEWIS W. HINE, who is home from the New East, will give us next month another photo story of how these uprooted peoples lived en route.

"ON THEIR OWN"

TWO war orphans, father and mother having died in Bulgaria. They had traveled to southern Macedonia, and were still going strong, cared for by any other refugees who happened to take a fancy to them. Here in Skoplie they were under the care of the Red Cross.

how far they had come the man confusingly answered, "Two days by horse and cart or three by train!" Two smaller photographs positioned at the lower, outer corners reiterate the "homeward" theme. On the left, a group is pictured at the bow of a ship; on the right, Greek refugees sitting in a plaza await transportation.

The photographs on the last pages of the substory are entitled "Ten Years From Home and Still Refugees." Two small, overlapping panoramic pictures introduce it. The top one is a long-distance landscape photograph that shows a refugee village established by the Greek government for Greeks who had escaped Bulgarian persecution. The picture beneath it is a large group portrait of villagers. On the opposite page is a photograph of two young orphan boys that fills the space of that page. The caption reads: "Two war orphans, father and mother having died in Bulgaria. They had traveled to southern Macedonia, and were still going strong, cared for by any other refugees who happened to take a fancy to them. Here in Skoplie they were under the care of the Red Cross." The differences between Folks's language and Hine's is worth noting. Hine's original caption for the picture had read: "This is a type of child the American Red Cross is saving every day in Serbia. These two children are orphans, having to look out for themselves, their parents having died in Bulgaria. They are on the steps of the Kahn Kapan, formerly a Turkish Inn, now a hotel for refugees, who are coming back from Bulgaria to go on to their home."

While the holding power of the narration and singularity of theme carries the reader forward, the pictorial syntax of this spread is ambiguous. The size of the photographs is visually inconsistent, and, they seem to have no relationship to one another: oversized photographs occupy the top portion of the page (on pages 524–25) while tiny photographs appear to be floating at the bottom. The fourth page of the essay contains three small photographs arranged without any logic at all: the sequence contains a panorama of a Greek village that imparts no sense of scale; the second is a group portrait so small and with so many people that anyone beyond the first row is indistinguishable; the third is a barely readable photograph of Hine lurching forward to make a group portrait. Even in instances where the photographs are uncropped, they are too small and illegible to sustain the action of the spread.

"They Departed into Their Own Country" appeared the following month, on August 2, 1919. It was Hine's only photo essay that employed "flashlight" photographs, one on the introductory page and two interior shots on the pages immediately following. But, unlike the photographs he produced for the National Child Labor Committee, these pictures do not make reference to the symbolic and cleansing possibilities of "light."

The first part of the story described the housing shortage in Salonika, Greece. The photographs are arranged in a contiguous fashion to show interior and exterior places inhabited by refugees. The largest photograph in the spread is on the right side of the page and serves as a partial centerfold—the action of the photo carries over from one page to the other. Outside of a building are "A group of Jews and Greeks among the pillars of the ancient Mosque Pariskevi." Hundreds of families now occupied the mosque (a former church); blankets were draped from beams to set off the living areas of individual families. Beneath the photograph of the mosque is a picture of a young girl at "a temporary altar of the Greek faith."

The syntactical arrangement of the photographs on the left also explores the inside–outside relationship. One features "another group of Greek refugees in an ancient Greek church"; a large family is huddled together beneath an archway, a single garment of clothing hanging on a pole above them. Below that photograph is one of a "homeless Jew cramped behind burlap curtains in a synagogue." An elderly woman's head emerges from a curtain as the flashlight goes off, over-illuminating the foreground of the picture but insufficiently lighting the background.

In its last two pages the story continues to explore the subject of "squatters" in the form of subcellar dwellings, outdoor "campsites," and makeshift tents that refugees resorted to in Serbia. In some ways these pictures recall the images of refugees fleeing Paris during the war; they have an intimate and unobtrusive feeling of a stressful, drama-laden moment. The photographs on the top of the page are contact print size (4x5 inches) and are visually balanced by the size and organization of text and photographs at the bottom. The top area displays a photograph of a mother and daughter who appear in the "doorway" of their subcellar dwelling; on the left a group of Serbian refugees cook food over a fire. (Figure 31)

On the bottom right is a photograph of a "RC worker at Skoplye giving some small Macedonian Serbs their first bath." While this photograph directly documented the Red Cross at work, it has a lyrical, somewhat steamy quality made palpable by the

WITH not even a roof over their heads, these families were finding their way back home on foot from northern Serbia where the Austrians and Germans had sent them to produce food for the enemy. Here they were at Grdjelitza, a little town half way home. It was one of the stopping points for the motor trucks by which the French and English were vainly trying to maintain freight transportation through Serbia.

At the right, a smiling family in a tent typical of hundreds of shelters, patched together from every sort of rags and tatters. When these people reach home, it will not be home, but simply ruins. They will have to begin all over again. Their children must still carry the load: the Child's Burden will be the theme of Mr. Hine's next series in the SURVEY for Sept. 6.

SUB-CELLAR dwellings in the ruins of the burned district of Salonika. Fifteen months after the great fire they were still in use because of the shortage of building material, of funds, and the indifference of the war-plagued inhabitants. In one of these small caves were crowded two families, including fourteen persons, three of whom were ill. Water stood a foot deep on the floor in rainy weather and the ceiling was continually caving in.

At the left, a Red Cross worker at Skoplye giving some small Macedonian Serbs their first bath. The Red Cross used an old Turkish inn, the Khan Kapan, for a refugee hotel and equipped it with odds and ends. Even petrol cans had to serve as bathtubs. Making bricks without straw was an everyday experience for Red Cross workers in Serbia—and they did it.

F I G U R E   31

All of the European photo stories featured cropped
enlargements of Hine's original photographs, such as the
two top pictures reproduced here. (SWHA)

Kids is Kids

THE little Greek girl in Salonika, carrying home a sack of food that has been given her; the Belgian children to whom the sight of ruined homes has become habitual; the little French "gamine" critically examining her American-grown cereal—little do they know how closely they share a common human experience.

SERBIAN children in makeshift clothes; a Bohemian infant, wrapped by his hollow-cheeked mother in an old sack; little Italy, courageous though underfed; and young Turkey, smiling though barely covered in decency— all part of the great procession of suffering childhood.

F I G U R E   32

"Kids is Kids" is the best example of Hine's postwar photo stories. It appeared in an article by Folks entitled "The War and the Children," along with other photographs by Hine. (SWHA)

soft focus of the picture. The photograph on the opposite page is of a family of Jews happily posing outside their tent.

Although individual photographs in this piece are not Hine's most forceful, "They Departed into Their Own Country" is one of the more accomplished collaborative stories. The understatement of Hine's photographs is echoed in Folks's simple, descriptive captions; the photo story itself reinforces the complementary relationship between photograph and text. Folks recognized the inherent beauty and value of Hine's photographs: "These pictures are history. From them you can reconstruct in imagination a little of what the war has meant to refugees, of whom . . . five million are slowly finding their way home."

One of the most imaginative uses of the photo story format occurred in "The War and the Children," the last of the reconstruction articles, which was featured in *The Survey* on November 8, 1919. However, this particular piece was not a collaboration. The first part of the story contained an article by Folks, excerpted from *The Human Costs of the War*, which included several photographs by Hine. In a letter from Folks to Kellogg about this story, he instructed Kellogg that "Hine can select the pictures for it."

Following the article was an independent, two-page photo story of Hine's entitled "Kids is Kids." (Figure 32) "Kids" is a well-thought-out photo story, one in which the syntax of the photographs works together to underscore the intention of the story: that the innocent spirit of kids enables them to survive.

The story featured seven photographs of various sizes arranged in a dynamic double-page spread. Like *The Survey's* other photo stories, some of the photographs are unusually large. The text, however, occupies two small portions of the page. Visually, except for the title, it almost appears as an afterthought.

Hine used two images to frame the essay. On the left is a horizontal photograph of a serious young girl carrying a sack of goods, and on the far right of the spread is a full-length portrait, laid out vertically, of a smiling Greek boy who is dressed in rags. The girl looks directly at the camera; the boy gazes off camera but into the action of the story. The photographs have been cropped to accentuate visual details such as the size of the girl's sack and the motley appearance of the boy.

The photograph of the girl has been cut out in such a way that the title of the essay literally appears over her shoulder. The negatives from this series are 4x5 inches; the photograph of the girl has been cropped and enlarged so that the child appears proportionately larger than she is. The photograph of the boy evokes a cheerful feeling, despite his disheveled state. Also, the boy's smile is engaging and his body posture relaxed.

The essay includes the only Belgian photograph—of school girls jauntily walking down the street—juxtaposed to a picture of a young French child eating cereal. On the following page is a totem-pole-like arrangement of three youngsters squinting into the sun as they pose for Hine, a young Serbian mother and her infant daughter, and another candid photograph of a smiling young Italian girl (whom Hine referred to as "little mother and her charges,") standing on the railway tracks bidding Hine goodbye. Hine focused on children who had survived the trauma of the war; as a result, the mood of this piece is hopeful and optimistic.

"Kids" also serves to illustrate the different positions from which Hine made his photographs. In one he crouches to portray an infant surrounded by two siblings, in another he photographed from a train window above a group of Italian street kids, and in a third he holds the camera at a very low angle to capture a little girl, her head no higher than the chair alongside her, eating.

A portion of the caption addresses the fact that "little do they know how closely they share a common human experience." Indeed, the shared experiences of people and children, their "common emancipation," culminate in the European photos and emerge as the subtext of Hine's body of work from 1904 to 1919.

There is, however, one group of European photographs Hine produced that deviates from this general theme. They are the pictures he made upon returning from the Balkan Survey in February 1919. While the sequence of images illustrates his general conception of a photo story, they also appear to have been a diversion from the taxing emotional experiences of the campaign. Produced in the winter of 1919, the group consists of twenty-two posed photographs of an American doughboy. They form the basic elements for a photo essay about what an American soldier with a surfeit of recreational time does in postwar Paris.[26]

"Mud ankle-deep in Serbia made the trip
for members of the survey not an easy one.
Here they are pushing the Red Cross camion
out of the mire on the road between Vranja
and Grdelitza." (LC)

"Refugees on top of boxcars, exposed to
all kinds of weather, returning to their homes.
Strumitza. December 1918." (LC)

"Refugees following the railroad track en
route to Grdelitza, Serbia. December 1918."
(LC)

"Left to right: Boy carrying home work,
delivery boy, and youthful water carrier.
November 1918." (LC)

C320

X.-320

"Refugee family en route somewhere. Skoplie, Serbia." (CAH)

"'Wuxtrie,' the newsie of Belgrade.
November 1918." (LC)

X-323

"Street beggars. Belgrade." (CAH)

"Washing fruits and vegetables at a public spigot. Italian tenements adjacent to St. Peter's, Rome." (LC)

"A 'little mother' and her charges. These little helpers are very common sights on the streets of Tarente. November 1918." (LC)

"A glimpse of Picadilly Circus. Salonika. December 1918." (LC)

"A milkman of Salonika making the rounds
of his customers. December 1918." (LC)

Y-94

"Rapid transit in Belgrade, Serbia." (LC)

"A Turkish milkman and a candidate for the 'white wings.' Salonika. December 1918."
(LC)

"Returned refugees to Pordenone showing girl of nineteen between two women of sixty-four (in front) and seventy-four (behind)."
(CAH)

"A woman, whose husband was wounded, traveling by donkey car with her mother and three children. They were driven out of St. Nicholo by the Austrians, are now on the way to Belfior and San Dona del Piave. Their only food for days was yellow corn. November 1918." (LC)

X-19

X-19

"In the public market at Athens, the animals are killed while you wait. This small boy is the butcher's assistant. November 1918." (LC)

"Mother carrying her sick boy about the streets of Belgrade in search of relief." (LC)

"A Macedonian Turk carrying home his
bread supply. Salonika. December 1918."
(LC)

X-68

"A street type at Salonika. December 1918."
(LC)

"Shepherdess with stick. Bralo, Greece." (LC)

X-241

"A rag picker of Belgrade. December 1918."
(LC)

X-241

"A Christmas street fiddler. Belgrade.
December 1918." (LC)

X-350

"Giuseppe Ugesti. Italian soldier in 223rd Infantry. He was an Austrian prisoner at Milowitz (reported to be very bad) for ten months. He is now confined to his bed with tuberculosis. January 1919." (LC)

"Every home has its own disinfecting plant.
Refugees at Lescowatz, Serbia. December
1918." (LC)

X-166

"A Turkish beggar and child. Salonika." (LC)

X-92

"A Turkish boy in Salonika. He has just been to the American Red Cross and has obtained food, hence the smile at the cameraman. December 1918." (LC)

"On the way to market at Semendria.
December 1918." (LC)

"A young shepherdess. Greece. December 1918." (LC)

"No—this Turkish boy is not a girl. He wears these braids in memory of his two sisters who died. Skoplie. December 1918." (LC)

"Character study, old man. Salonika, Greece"
(CAH)

X-103

"Blind street beggar. Belgrade." (CAH)

"Refugees cooking meal on road to
Grdelitza, Serbia." (CAH)

"Dwellers in the subcellar of the ruins of Salonika. Eighteen persons (two families) live in this, and their chief occupation seems to be picking out nut-meats for the market. December 1918." (LC)

"Subcellar dwellings in the burned district. In one of these caves fourteen people live, representing two families, and three of them are ill. The roof caved in, dropping dirt and brick on them. The water is at times a foot deep and has to be bailed out. Salonika. November 1918." (LC)

X132

"Greek refugees who were driven out of eastern Macedonia (Seres and Dama) into Serbia (near Nish) by the Bulgars, now returning to their homes. They live now in an abandoned building which is in a very bad state of repair. Lescowatz. December 1918."
(LC)

"Interior of a ruined synagogue, housing nineteen families. There are twenty-two synagogues in the city of Salonika being used in this way. December 1918." (LC)

"A corner in the basement of one of the ruined buildings of Salonika. Nine people (two families) live in this small space. December 1918." (LC)

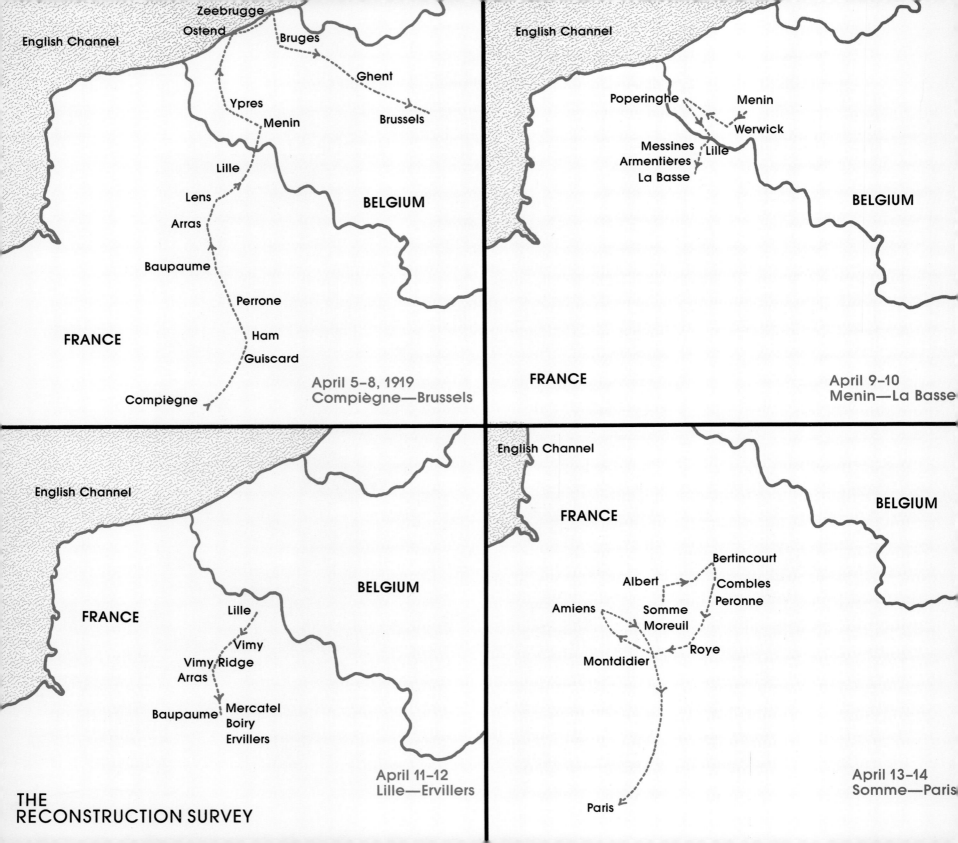

English Channel
Zeebrugge
Ostend
Bruges
Ghent
Ypres
Menin
Brussels
Lille
Lens
Arras
BELGIUM
Baupaume
Perrone
FRANCE
Ham
Guiscard
April 5–8, 1919
Compiègne—Brussels
Compiègne

English Channel
Poperinghe
Menin
Werwick
Messines
Armentières
Lille
La Basse
BELGIUM
FRANCE
April 9–10
Menin—La Basse

English Channel
FRANCE
BELGIUM
Lille
Vimy
Vimy Ridge
Arras
Baupaume
Mercatel
Boiry
Ervillers
April 11–12
Lille—Ervillers

THE RECONSTRUCTION SURVEY

English Channel
FRANCE
BELGIUM
Bertincourt
Albert
Combles
Peronne
Amiens
Somme
Moreuil
Roye
Montdidier
Paris
April 13–14
Somme—Paris

More than two months after the Special Survey team had returned to Paris, on April 4, 1919, Lieutenant Colonel Folks, Captain Hine, and Mr. G.C. Clark, a stenographer, set out on an arduous ten-day survey of northern France and Belgium. As Folks explained in his book, their purpose was "to see the conditions of housing, food and employment at this very early stage of reconstruction." Six months after the Armistice had been declared, about "one-fifth of the refugees had returned and more were coming every day." Most returned to destroyed homes, villages, and ravaged land.

The photographs that Hine made on the second part of the Special Survey Mission were of former sites of the war's fiercest fighting. They depict reconstruction from another angle, to show the courageous efforts of returning refugees to reestablish their lives with and without the succor of the American Red Cross. They represent his final group of European photographs.

Due to the fast-paced nature of the trip Hine's emphasis was not on rendering the individual but on providing a panorama of the effects of war. In this way, the northern European photographs are different from the Balkan images. Few reveal the poignant, candid scenes of Italians, Serbians, or Greeks engaged by his camera. Instead, many are long-distance shots of families reestablishing home life, although some have the modernist, dynamic thrust of Hine's eastern European images. Generally, however, there is an unsettling, remote feeling in these photographs underscored by the decimation of the surrounding landscape.

Civilians were slowly making their way home, but public transportation was still inadequate, and the winter thaw had made many of the roads impassable. Nevertheless, the Special Survey team traveled by automobile into some of the small towns hardest hit by the war. Unknowingly, the team had based its itinerary on a pre-wartime map of France and Belgium. (Figure 33) En route, it was soon discovered that several towns they had set out to survey had been completely leveled. Ironically, the survey that was planned conformed to a Belgium that no longer existed.

Folks's diary recounted their passage: "Left Paris in automobile at 7:45 for Belgium and northern France." On April 5, the men journeyed through twelve towns and villages, from Compiègne to La Panne; on April 6, they surveyed several destroyed towns on the western front and they "crossed the old front of La Panne a few miles out of Belgian and French trenches a mile or more apart, [and] a flooded area between"; on April 7, they visited the "destroyed factories of Mr. Boel of La Louviere"; on April 8, they were in Louvain where Hine (using a 5x7 Graflex) "took several photos showing progress toward reconstruction"; on April 9, they entered Ghent, Belgium, and subsequently surveyed nineteen towns that comprised a "tour of the devastated region, observed especially the number of people who had returned, and how they were housed, etc."; on April 10, they returned to France to report findings to American Red Cross workers in the nine towns contiguous with Armentières, where "Miss Harris, Mrs. Goodale, Lieutenant Milner and Captain Moffatt dined with us." They continued on April 11 and visited the factory districts of Lille and Lens with Mrs. Goodale, and "took a considerable number of very interesting pictures of people living in improvised quarters on the battle front at the foot of Vimy Ridge." On the morning of April 12, it rained, and they drove on to the villages of St. Catherine and St. Nicholas, in the district of Arras, and surveyed six villages before they reached Amiens.

On April 13 they resumed at a quicker pace, with Mrs. Stuart, a delegate to the Department of the Somme, and visited twelve towns. On April 14, the last day of the survey, with Mrs. Stuart still accompanying them, Hine took pictures of Thennes, Moreuil, Montdidier, Bouillancourt, and the American Cemetery at Cantigny. In total the group visited seventy-eight towns in ten days, and Hine made approximately four hundred negatives.

Thematically, the northern European photographs convey a dialectic of dissolution and reconstruction. The photographs have less formal variation than the pictures and portraits Hine made in eastern Europe. There the images are tightly organized to emphasize a group or individual subject. In France and Belgium there is a greater feeling of space, but it is not a comforting one: a family situated alongside a makeshift dwelling typically occupies just a portion of the frame, while the surrounding area reveals a frightening expanse of emptiness.

The fact that Hine exclusively used a larger, 5x7 inch Graflex in some way explains the different look of these later photographs.

Yet, there are other factors that account for their indeterminate sense of space. Given the accelerated pace of the journey and that Hine was often making photos from a moving car, there was insufficient time to get close to a subject. Nevertheless, when possible, Hine thought through a strategy to present the panorama in vivid—if appalling—detail.

Generally, the photographs are characterized by a well-defined spatial tension between the center of the frame, where people appear, and a background void. Because of the distancing of the human figure these pictures are less suitable to the photo story format. Indeed, many of the photographs work best in paired units that illustrate a dialectic of destruction–reconstruction. This coupling of photographs was used in "Peace-Time Pioneers," an article by Folks that appeared in a magazine called *The World's Work*.

According to its publisher, Walter H. Page, *The World's Work* was a corporate magazine that aimed "to report and to interpret representative activities of our time and give the reader a well-proportioned knowledge of what sort of things are happening in the world." The magazine's unique slant was that it offered articles of an upbeat or "inspirational" nature oriented to the corporate executive. (Figure 34) For Folks the "courage and strong heart" of northern European refugees returning home was such an inspirational story. In expressive detail, he recaptured the turmoil in which families were forced to flee, their ensuing separation, sickness, fear, and problems in resettlement. Now that the war was over, the refugees' journey home after an absence of four-and-a-half years was depicted in "Peace-Time Pioneers" and depended on Hine's photographs to show "with a wealth of convincing detail the picturesque, pathetic and grotesque expedients to which these resourceful peacetime pioneers in the war zone have resorted."

After returning to the United States, Hine personally employed this serial relationship with photographs to render an elderly couple's efforts at beginning anew. In the first photograph the woman is featured alone and at a more intimate distance than in virtually any other Special Survey picture. For her, having one's picture taken is a formal occasion, and so she removes her

ONE OF THE GOVERNMENT BARRACKS
This house is one of the best that has been erected to alleviate the homeless condition of the people of Perenchies

THE HOME-COMING

F I G U R E 34

Hine's northern European Survey work was primarily used to illustrate Folks's written material. The fast-paced nature of this second mission imparts a panoramic sense of reconstruction efforts underway throughout France and Belgium. (NYPL)

FRANCE

W-167 and W-168a. TOGETHER. Jan-1919

This aged couple have returned ~~together~~ and are occupying their former home, inspite of ~~its shortcomings~~ the French prejudice against excessive ventilation. ~~Their former home~~ in Thennes, near Amiens, ~~was ruined during~~ caused by the great German drive of March and April of 1918. The character of these French people is well shown in the grandmotherly face.

By Hine for Amer. Red Cross.

77:175:11

77:175:12

F I G U R E 35

Upon returning to the United States Hine continued to experiment with the combination of serial photographs and text. This diptych is from his personal archives and is mislabeled "January 1919." (GEH)

eyeglasses. In the contiguous candid photograph, the couple is dwarfed by their "home," a skeleton of bare beams and lathing. Hine's caption, which has been revised in his own handwriting, alludes to "the character of these French people well shown in the grandmotherly face." (Figure 35) (Note that the diptych has been inaccurately dated "January 1919.")

Unlike the Balkan Survey work, where Hine usually photographed alone, the three men, and whoever else joined them, apparently were inseparable. There are several candid photographs of Folks talking with refugees, as well as pictures of the Red Cross dispensing mattresses to queued-up French civilians.

Although Hine had made a brief, wartime tour through northern France in the summer of 1918, Folks had been confined to Paris for most of the war. His article in *The World's Work* was about "the conditions in devastated northern France and Belgium faced by returning refugees," and evokes the visceral shock of seeing the physical destruction of the western front for the first time. On the second survey he perceived the magnitude of the civilian population's needs: "In the fastest auto we traveled for ten days from early morning until dark . . . and saw nothing but devastation. . . . The very magnitude of it paralyzes even the mere effort to describe it, to say nothing of rebuilding. . . . Repeatedly, as we approached a town we thought, 'This place seems to have escaped.' The buildings appeared to be standing, yet as we entered the town and went into the buildings, we found only a ghost of a city."

Hine's images of destroyed towns and ravaged landscapes graphically picture the topographical devastation Folks described. However, both Folks and Hine felt a deep admiration for the civilians, one that is somehow insufficiently conveyed in the photos. By earlier highlighting a medium-distance shot of a Serbian refugee as a symbol of yesterday's losses and today's hope, for example, Hine created an optimistic picture of the war's aftermath. But, in northern Europe, long-shot studies predominate and the subjects are distant. Thus, Hine's northern European survey style was a deviation from his usual working method. Because the team worked quickly and often viewed the landscape and returning refugees from a car, Hine's photographs show little, if any,

detail. Furthermore, when the three men did stop, the brief amount of time spent at a site did not encourage the use of a close-up. Although Hine typically avoided imagery in which a person or group was pictured at an inaccessible distance from his camera, most of the photographs show people in long shot, such as civilian families rebuilding their homes. Also, since the photographs were compositionally standardized, it was difficult to arrange them in sequences of establishing shot, close-up, etc. Hine apparently felt this lack of formal narrative progression; with one exception these pictures were not employed in his post-war photo stories.

Given the rapidity with which the team surveyed a village, Hine's photographs have the appearance of "shooting from the hip." In some pictures he photographs spontaneously from afar without making any personal contact. In the picture showing the "ruined portion of Louvain," the foreground is filled with the rubble of the war. Seven children, tiny figures in relation to the buildings behind them, casually peer at him from a distance. Other photographs have the appearance of being made "on the road." In one, "the heart of the Somme battlefield" occupies the foreground of the picture and two small figures in the distance stand atop the rubble of their home. In others a handwritten notice, "*Maison Habite*," was the only sign that a decimated building was occupied.

Folks noted in his diary the particular villages where the team stopped to "take several pictures." In these photographs, the men left the car to chat with villagers. The photographs are often posed, medium-distance shots that show families at work. There are several photographs of inventive shelters, such as the one of "an entrance to the quarters of a thrifty couple in Lens" who occupy a cellar dwelling. In a picture such as this, where the man and woman are impeccably dressed and pose gracefully before the entranceway of their home, the photographs have some of the trenchant qualities so powerful in the Balkan Survey work.

Another variation in the northern European work involved picturing the challenges to survival. In the eastern European photographs, men, women, and children were often pitted against hunger, disease, and suffering; in the northern European photographs the overwhelming physical destruction of home, land, and

F I G U R E 36
A Hine photograph that was slit into two for dramatic effect.
(NYPL)

animals emerges as a metaphor of the loss of self. As "Peace-Time Pioneers" shows, the landscape refugees returned to alternated between one "ready for the harvest" and one "where the land is a succession of shell holes." Like the refugees in Greece and Serbia, families devised creative ways of survival. One family who returned to the Vimy Ridge occupied a "dugout . . . during the time their house is being built out of the corrugated iron in the vicinity," and casually pose alongside it to have their picture taken.

In a departure from Hine's humanistic vision, several of the photographs contain no people at all. In "Peace-Time Pioneers," two photographs show an empty vista where "War's Wilderness—Reaches the Horizon." A landscape of destroyed "tanks, shell holes filled with water, and ruined barbed wire entanglements" is the "Site of the former village of Hooge near Ypres, Belgium. . . . The ground is treacherous with mines and unexploded ammunition of every sort." (Figure 36) (Other photographs, which are part of the Reconstruction Survey but do not appear in "Peace-Time Pioneers," index the passage of English-speaking troops. In one a posted sign in the foreground of a desolate landscape reads "This *was* Villers-Carbonnel.")

Perhaps the most uncharacteristic feature of the northern European work is the relative absence of children. In cases where Hine did make contact with a child, as in the picture of a bandaged boy standing atop a heap of mortar, the child is not in close-up. In others, children are with their families and gardening, building, or cleaning. One exception is the street photograph of Belgian school girls. (Figure 32)

The photographs of Belgium and France were used with less frequency in Folks's material, too. Although nine appeared in "Peace-Time Pioneers," only ten appeared in *The Human Costs of the War*. And, unlike the Balkan Survey prints, all of the Reconstruction Survey photographs were printed full frame (uncropped).

Hine's northern European photographs were primarily reproduced in Folks's book. Twenty-eight of his Balkan and European photographs appeared in *The Human Costs of the War*. The manuscript went through several major revisions to ultimately focus on the civilian populations of Europe and chronicled the effects of war on "property and human life," to show "that both sides

MANY HANDS
But even so, it is not light work when you are building shelters in the ruins of Lens, France.

NOT MUCH LEFT
But even in these ruins this mother and four children, who have been refugees two years and a half, find a shelter.

F I G U R E 37
Folks's book, *The Human Costs of the War*, employed twenty-eight of Hine's Balkan and northern European photographs. (NYPL)

waged an effective war." While the credit, "Illustrated with Photographs by Lewis W. Hine, American Red Cross, Special Survey Mission," appears on the title page of the book, Hine apparently had no influence on the arrangement of the pictures. (Figure 37)

The photographs appeared in standard fashion, that is, photographs and captions were contiguous with a page of text. Usually, two photographs appeared on the right-hand side of the page, one on top of the other, and photographs of France and Belgium were not interspersed with those of the first survey. Also, posed photographs appear on the same page as candid ones. Other than survey conformity—photographs of the same mission are doubled on the page—there is no implied visual relationship between the images.

Hine and Folks obviously felt the need to pursue additional survey work in France and Belgium, because on April 27 a larger group attempted to leave Paris on a second leg of a Reconstruction tour. This time Hine, Folks, and Clark were accompanied by Folks's family—his daughters Evelyn and Gertrude and Mrs. Folks. They set out again by automobile to travel through Compiègne and then on to Ribecourt, Noyon, Chauny, Teginier, La Fere, and Laon, villages that Folks and Hine had not surveyed on the earlier trip. In the evening the automobile broke down. On the following day they were unsuccessful at fixing the broken auto spring and took a train back to Paris.

Within two months both Hine and Folks would return to the United States, Folks to his home base in New York and Hine to Washington, D.C., where he worked for the publicity department at the national headquarters of the American Red Cross. (Figure 38) Ironically, as restrictions regarding wartime and postwar imagery were lifted, Hine's images were not utilized to their fullest: only a dozen of his photos actually appeared in Red Cross publications.

FIGURE 38
This undated silhouette of Hine, created by Homer Folks, was probably given to him as a memento of their tour in Europe. (GEH)

Six months after the Armistice was declared, the American Red Cross had almost completely withdrawn its "armies" from Belgium, France, and Italy and had begun to send workers to Russia (Siberia), Turkey, Poland, Rumania, and Serbia. Its articles urged readers toward increased giving because "Never before has the idealism of America been able to express itself in practical deeds." Given the revised orientation of Red Cross reconstruction efforts, the photographs that Hine made in Italy, Greece, France, and Belgium were, for the most part, no longer germane to current efforts.

To further American support for its activities *The Red Cross Magazine* instituted a monthly feature, beginning in October 1919, called "The March of the Red Cross," which was "a continued story of accomplishment; each month's chapter based on recent cables, letters and reports of workers in many parts of the world." This first issue featured a cropped Hine photograph of a young Greek shepherdess, posed in situ. In the context of the article it is an obfuscating contradiction of Red Cross propaganda and goals. The young girl pictured is not receiving any food or assistance, nor does she appear to be in need of any. Nevertheless, the photograph is inset onto a picture of a group of orphans who are eating at a table; concomitantly, a Red Cross worker ladles out soup to a child whose posture vividly recalls one of Hine's early National Child Labor Committee pictures. Furthermore, the photograph has been appropriated to symbolize American Red Cross work in Poland. The caption alludes to the young shepherdess: "Today there are four million destitute people in Poland. Here is a type of child the Red Cross is fighting to save." Hine did not receive a credit for the photograph.[27]

Just as Paul Kellogg envisioned *The Survey* as a unique forum to address the postwar role of the United States in world affairs, so did Red Cross executives view their magazine. By 1920 the format went through stylistic changes to better illustrate the organization's programs. Above the title a heading was introduced that read, "The Magazine of A Better America."[28] In addition to featuring its monthly report, the magazine emerged as a principal vehicle in which to articulate the role of the Red Cross as "a new and great force in American life . . . and give a 'true picture'

of the spirit of America at work." Its August 1920 issue also presented articles by a former muckraker, Ida Tarbell, and another monthly feature entitled "Better America" that presented healing, "true stories of people and things that will strengthen your faith in your country."

The journal continued to highlight European reconstruction projects and added "Glimpses of the New Red Cross" in April 1920 that presented photographs by Lewis Hine showing "the variety of work that the Red Cross is now doing in our country." On assignment for the magazine as its staff photographer, he traveled to Long Island and upstate New York, New Jersey, Massachusetts, and Illinois to show "how the different branches are using their war experiences to guide them in these days of peace."

Although it is unclear how much influence Hine had on the design of his pictures and text, his signature is evident in some of the reproductions. Pictorially, the photographs were arranged in a mirrorlike design of six to ten images per page—those on the left reflecting the same size and shape as those on the right. In the June 1920 issue he refers to them as his "picture-serial," which has the "reality and conviction of a moving picture." Hine also wrote long captions for these photo spreads that managed to combine some edge of his own voice—clear, concise, descriptive—in tandem with the unctuous language of the Red Cross. By August 1920, however, he would no longer be credited as "our staff photographer," and his photographs would not reappear in Red Cross fund-raising publications until 1931.

With few exceptions, the last twenty years of Hine's life represent a protracted period of career frustrations that counterpoint the productive days with his European colleagues. In conversations later in life—nearly two years before the United States entered the second World War—Hine did not favor the European photographs. Nevertheless, they emerge as some of the most important photographs of his career and embody a theme that has pervaded the pictorial press since the second World War: humanistic coverage of the social issues relating to war and peace. While one may take exception to his occasional "corniness," his work set precedents in its nonsensational, nonexploitative interpretation of human misery. His subjects are revealed with a reverence for the horrors they have endured and tacitly shared with him. In a sense, Hine's lifelong program of reducing the story to "the character in the cast" gives his work its dimensionality and extraordinary resonance. Indeed, had he lived to see the new photojournalism emerging during the second World War, he may have taken special pride in the ways in which his European work foreshadowed these practices.

By 1939 Europe was engulfed in another great war, and a wave of emigrants entered the United States. Photographers and picture editors responsible for such sophisticated illustrated weeklies as *Die Berliner Illustrirte Zeitung* and *Münchner Illustrirte Presse* fled Hitler and journeyed to England and the United States. The American publisher Henry Luce, who had made a successful venture of *Fortune* magazine, had a plan of developing a picture magazine in the United States that would feature news photographs in stylish graphic designs. He called the magazine *Life*. Although *Life* was hailed and promoted as an American invention, in fact, Luce had modeled his idea on the European photo stories edited and designed by Kurt Korff and photographed by Alfred Eisenstadt and Martin Munkacsi.[29] By November 1936 he had test-marketed and published *Life*, which was an instant hit. Within six months a competitive journal called *Look* was also published. Hine followed the development of these new picture magazines with great interest, but, in 1937, differentiated his own vision by saying, "I am not a bit satisfied to sacrifice pictorial value to the fetish of having a unified thread . . . (The weekly magazines do that so beautifully!)" (S.W.H.A.)

In 1938, two years before Hine's death, Elizabeth McCaus-land, a teacher, writer, and photography critic, "rediscovered" him. She, along with the photographer Berenice Abbott and a host of photo-world luminaries including Alfred Stieglitz, organized a retrospective at New York City's Riverside Museum in January 1939. In her catalogue essay for the exhibition, as well as in subsequent articles for photography and social welfare magazines, and in her columns for the *Springfield Republican*, McCaus-land praised Hine for dissolving the boundaries between social and artistic photography. Addressing his pioneering work in *The Complete Photographer* as "anticipating the current trend for a closer liaison between photographer and writer," she was the first writer to recognize his innovative contributions to the rise of photojournalism in the United States.

In addition to organizing the Hine retrospective, McCaus-land, and her work, induced the editors of the *Survey Graphic* to formally laud Hine's visionary use of the social photograph and development of the photo story format. Paul Kellogg's editorial reads in part: "Thirty years before the picture magazines (with their sequences of pictorial documents of our time) appeared on the newsstands, Lew Hine, pioneer sharpshooter, embellished our pages with his photographs." Unfortunately, efforts at resurrecting Hine's career did not reach beyond a community already appreciative of his work. Hine, who had contacted the editors of *Life* for assignments, had written to McCausland: "The LIFE-guards are keeping me on the string,—they say they want to use my stuff in Labor Day No., but how much to believe them I do not know." Hine did have an opportunity to do a photo story for *Fortune*, but not for *Life*. He died in poverty and neglect in 1940.

"On the road to Arras and Bapaume.
France." (CAH)

"Under the arch. This arch of a cellar does temporarily for all household needs until something better can be found. Moreuil, France." (GEH)

W178

"Maison Habité. Hut made of corrugated
sheet iron, paper and wood." (C.A.H.)

"This British military hut shelters a refugee mother and her family on the scene of some of the fiercest fighting of the war, not far from Ypres." (LC)

"This returned refugee, a mason by trade, is building a very comfortable dwelling in the midst of an area of complete devastation. Note brick sides and thatched roof. A tiny garden surrounds the house. Near Kemmel Hill, Belgium. April 1919." (LC)

"A portion of the site of the village of Hooge, Belgium, showing the present condition of the site of a hard-fought battle. The land is one succession of shell craters now filled with water. The ruins of Ypres are in the extreme distance. French civilians are repairing the road, a very hazardous occupation, on account of the abundance of unexploded ammunition." (LC)

"The home of the poilu and his baby. Moreuil, France, between Amiens and Montdidier. The final rush of the Germans in the spring of 1918 was stopped 1/2 mile beyond this point. The rough shack over a former cellar shelters a demobilized poilu, his wife and child, and grandfather. The only opening is through the door in which may be seen the poilu's face." (GEH)

W170

"General view of the ruins of Combles, France, population of 1,300. No refugees have returned to this region. This picture gives a good impression of the utter desolation of the Somme battlefield." (LC)

Combles

"The type of building most frequently seen
in the ruined portion of Louvain, Belgium."
(CAH)

"General view of Lens, France. April 11,
1919." (LC)

"General view facing on Place de la Republique in central portion of Armentières, France. In the foreground, a boy who has been injured by playing with powder from unexploded ammunition. In a nearby village, three children had been killed in this manner in three separate homes. April 1919."
(LC)

RC-8912

1. In fact, given Hine's refusal to adapt to the hedonistic spirit of the 1920s and the confluence of his social ideals and the church's, he may have undertaken minor free-lance assignments for its audio-visual department. Unfortunately, without any supporting documentation, attributing additional pictures to Hine would involve a good deal of speculation.

2. Although Gutman's text was instrumental in helping me track down the materials, all of the European photographs in her book were cropped so that the "X" and "W" codes did not appear in the reproduced image.

3. These photographs, numbering 251 prints and 289 negatives and fac-simile negatives, represent a portion of the work donated to the International Museum of Photography at George Eastman House by the Photo League after Hine's death. Many of the European prints are multiple copies of the same negative. In addition, G.E.H. houses 231 negatives and 149 prints from Hine's series on the Army and Navy training camps.

4. While some conservators have remarked about the poor technical quality of Hine's prints, they were not usually produced with "permanence" in mind. Indeed, many of his early photographs, especially those made for the National Child Labor Committee, were printed for reproduction purposes, not the fine art marketplace. This may explain why so many were insufficiently fixed and washed.

5. Immigration was treated in the February 1904 edition of *Charities*, but, as Clarke Chambers has written, it offered "a number of familiar stereotypes." *Paul U. Kellogg and The Survey*, (Minneapolis: University of Minnesota Press, 1971), page 100.

6. For two excellent analyses of Riis's work, see Sally Stein, "Making Connections with the Camera: Photography and Social Mobility in the Career of Jacob Riis," *Afterimage* (May 1983), pages 9–16; and Maren Stange, "Gotham's Crime and Misery, Ideology and Entertainment in Jacob Riis's Lantern Slide Exhibitions," *Views: The Journal of Photography in New England* (Spring 1987), pages 7–11.

7. In these cases, paints and inks were applied to fill in shadow areas and generalize facial details. See *McCall's*, vol. 43, no. 1, pages 14–15.

8. Mary Panzer's recent scholarship has dealt with a group of contemporaneous photographers whose work Stieglitz did not endorse. See, "Beauty and Utility: Rudolf Eikemeyer in the Gilded Age," *Views: The Journal of Photography in New England*, vol. 7, no. 3 (Spring 1986), pages 8–11; and Russell Hart, "The Outsiders," a review of "Pictorialism: A Symposium on Art Photography," vol. 8, no. 3 (Spring 1987), pages 4–5, 22.

9. According to Judith Mara Gutman, Hine never showed his work to Stieglitz. However, one of Hine's former students, Paul Strand, was accepted into the community, and *Camera Work*'s final issues were devoted to his work.

10. The other photographs featured in the journal are not credited to individual photographers although picture agencies and the Carnegie Steel Corporation are acknowledged.

11. That same issue featured a more compelling, independent photo story of Hine's about the children of immigrant workers entitled "Roving Children."

12. In part, this overly cautious attitude toward photography was a result of manipulation of photo data in daily newspapers. For a treatment of scandalous newspaper practices involving photographs, particularly in papers owned by William Randolph Hearst and Joseph Pulitzer, see *The Press & America* by Edwin Emery and Henry Smith Ladd.

13. Compare "A Child's Creed," pamphlet no. 234, page 10, with exhibit panel 3742. A self-possessed, smiling boy is depicted as the "normal child" (one not subjected to child labor) on the panel, but on page 10 of the pamphlet he symbolizes the child worker.

14. That same year, 1914, he also employed the hyphenated term "Photo-Story" for the first time in "Children or Cotton?—Raising the Question of Cotton Picking in Texas," *The Survey*, vol. 31 (February 7, 1914), pages 589–92.

15. See "In the Cool of the Evening," which features a street photograph of an Italian grandpa and his granddaughter contiguous with a landscape photograph of Van Cortlandt Park in *The Survey* (September 5, 1914), page 556.

16. For example, his name does not appear on the roster of the Henry Street Peace Committee.

17. Other than the two pieces described here, Hine's Time Exposures and photo stories strictly pertained to National Child Labor Committee issues and appeared regularly in *The Survey*. His work was also featured in *Outlook* and *International Socialist Review*.

18. In the other two essays, Hine intended to show the multiethnic make-up of the armed forces, but the effect of the stories in general is one of contrived superficiality, a manipulative distortion of army life that was curiously antithetical to Hine's position as a pacifist.

19. The second and third photographs in the sequence appeared in the

March 30, 1918, issue of *The Survey*, page 707. And, while *Life* magazine featured these same photographs in a spread about World War I in 1937, they did not appear in the popular press during or immediately after the war.

20. Later on, the horrors of the war were detailed by the sensational *Bryce Report*, which quoted Gleason at length. The *Report* contained no photographic evidence.

21. While the design and thrust of any photo story represents an orchestrated team effort of editor, photographer, and writer, the so-called "collaboration" between Folks and Hine is a curious one. In examining Folks's papers I found no evidence of any correspondence or meetings with Hine, let alone exchanges that pertained to the photo stories or Folks's book. Since Hine was still employed by the American Red Cross and based in Washington, D.C. (he also traveled extensively during this brief period), it appears as if he and Folks used Paul Kellogg as their contact.

22. Nevertheless, Folks's achievements at directing relief programs were officially acknowledged by the French Government when it named him a Chevalier of the Legion of Honor on May 26, 1919, just before he departed for the United States.

23. The title and manuscript were later changed to reflect Walter Page's view that "no one wants to hear a familiar horror story of the early parts of the war."

24. This is a particularly interesting photograph because it was made with Folks's assistance. His diary entry for Monday, December 23, reads: "This morning met Mr. Hine at 9:25 on the street by accident, and went with him to take pictures of Greek refugees. . . ." In the caption that reads: "Greek refugees huddled together in an old building at Lescowatz, Serbia. They had been driven out of Macedonia (Seres and Dana) into Serbia, near Nish, by the Bulgars. The building was in a deplorable state of repair and filth and mud were appalling. Families and cattle living together." This caption apparently was a collaborative effort: the last third of it, noting the "filth," "mud," and "families and cattle living together," has a decided Folksian tone.

25. All of the Italian photographs described in this paragraph are part of the Commission on Archives and History's photo collection.

26. There is, however, one group of European photographs Hine produced that deviates from this general theme. They are the pictures he made upon returning from the Balkan Survey in February 1919. While the sequence of images illustrates his general conception of a photo story, they also appear to have been a diversion from the taxing emotional experiences of the campaign. Produced in the winter of 1919, the group consists of twenty-two posed photographs of an American doughboy. They form the basic elements for a photo essay about what an American soldier with a surfeit of recreational time does in postwar Paris.

In each photo Hine directed a young doughboy through a series of predictable tableaux. In the first photo he arrives in Paris by train; later he makes a tourist trip to Notre Dame, then walks the snow-covered Bois du Boulogne. On the way back he asks directions from some other soldiers, one French, one American. Then we see him leaving a pissoir and hanging out for a smoke with his pals.

The photos of the soldier emerge as a schemata of a picture essay. Even though the photographs were apparently made over a period of several days, the overall impression is of "a day in the life" presentation. They are a closed series of pictures built around a simple principle: events are displayed in a succession of posed pictures that gives a linear sense of time. There is a lazy, humorous quality in the photos reflected in the self-consciousness of the soldier. Perhaps it is this feeling that brings to mind the type of pictures reproduced in *Everybody's Magazine*. Nevertheless, one photograph shows the scars of war: as the soldier leaves the pissoir the heavily bandaged face of a French *poilu* is visible in the left-hand portion of the frame. Perhaps Hine made these pictures on speculation, in the hope that *Everybody's* or another popular weekly would use them, but they were never published.

Twelve prints are in the Library of Congress, American Red Cross Collection, and ten are in the International Museum of Photography at George Eastman House.

27. Several months earlier, in *The Red Cross Magazine*'s May 1919 issue, vol. 14, no. 5, pages 9–15, several of Hine's prints were reproduced in an article entitled "The Awakening of the Children," by J.W. Studebaker.

28. At times—no doubt through a proofreading oversight—the heading inadvertently read "The Magazine of Better America." See the cover of the April 1920 issue.

29. Korff, who had been editor of *Die Berliner Illustrirte Zeitung*, met with Luce and Daniel Longwell, who became managing editor of *Life*, to make suggestions about their new journal. He recommended both Eisenstadt and Munkacsi as "camera reporters."

B O O K S

Brock, Peter. *Pacifism in the United States from the Colonial Era to the 1st World War.* Princeton, N.J.: Princeton University Press, 1968.

Brown, Theodore. *Margaret Bourke-White, Photojournalist.* Ithaca, N.Y.: Cornell University Press, 1972.

Chambers, Clarke A. *Paul U. Kellogg and the Survey, Voices for Social Welfare and Social Justice.* Minneapolis: University of Minnesota Press, 1971.

Chardin, Teilhard de. *The Heart of Matter.* English translation. New York: Harcourt Brace Jovanovich, A Helen and Kurt Wolff Book, 1978.

Creel, George. *How We Advertised America.* New York: Harper & Brothers Publishers, 1920.

——. *Rebel at Large.* New York: Putnam & Sons, 1947.

Curti, Merle. *Peace or War: The American Struggle 1636–1936.* New York: W. W. Norton & Co., 1936.

——. *The Growth of American Thought.* New York: Harper & Row, 1964.

DeBenedetti, Charles. *The Peace Reform Movement in American History.* Bloomington: Indiana University Press, 1980.

DeVoto, Bernard. *Mark Twain's America.* Cambridge: The Riverside Press and Houghton Mifflin Co., 1932.

DeWitt, Benjamin Parke. *The Progressive Movement.* New York: Macmillan Co., 1915.

Emerson, Ralph Waldo. *Addresses and Lectures.* Cambridge: The Riverside Press and Houghton Mifflin Co., 1837.

Emery, Edwin, ed. *The Story of America as Reported by Its Newspapers, 1690–1965.* New York: Simon & Schuster, 1965.

Emery, Edwin, and Smith, Henry Ladd. *The Press and America.* New York: Prentice-Hall, 1954.

Folks, Homer. *The Human Costs of the War.* New York: Harper & Brothers Publishers, 1920.

Frank, Waldo; Mumford, Lewis; Newman, Dorothy; et al., eds. *America & Alfred Stieglitz, a Collective Portrait.* Millerton, N.Y.: Aperture, 1975.

Freund, Gisèle. *Photography and Society.* Boston: David R. Godine, 1980.

Gidal, Tim. *Modern Photojournalism, Origin and Evolution 1910–1932.* New York: Macmillan Co., 1973.

Gilbo, Patrick F., ed. *The American Red Cross: The First Century, A Pictorial History.* New York: Harper & Row, 1981.

Gould, Lewis, and Greffe, Richard. *Photojournalist: The Career of Jimmy Hare.* New York: Harper & Bros., 1977.

Gutman, Judith Mara. *Lewis W. Hine and the American Social Conscience.* New York: Walker and Company, 1967.

Hicks, Wilson. *Words and Pictures: An Introduction to Photojournalism.* New York: Harper & Bros., 1952.

Homer, William Innes. *Alfred Stieglitz and the Photo-Secession.* Boston: Little, Brown & Co., A New York Graphic Society Book, 1983.

Kahan, Robert Sidney. "The Antecedents of American Photojournalism." Ph.D. diss., University of Wisconsin, 1969.

Kaplan, Justin. *Mark Twain and His World.* New York: Simon & Schuster, 1974.

——. *Walt Whitman: A Life.* New York: Simon & Schuster, 1980.

Kouwenhoven, John A. *Made in America: The Arts in Modern Civilization.* Garden City, N.Y.: Doubleday & Co., 1948.

Kwiat, J., and Turple, Mary C., eds. *Studies in American Culture.* Minneapolis: University of Minnesota Press, 1960.

Lewinski, Jorge. *The Camera at War: A History of War Photography from 1848 to the Present Day.* New York: Simon & Schuster, 1978.

Marchand, C. Roland. *The American Peace Movement and Social Reform, 1898–1918.* Princeton, N.J.: Princeton University Press, 1972.

McCabe, Lida Rose. *The Beginning of the Halftone : From the Notebooks of Stephen H. Horgan, "Dean of American Photoengravers."* Chicago: The Inland Printer, 1924.

McCausland, Elizabeth. *Lewis W. Hine Retrospective Catalogue.* New York: The Riverside Museum, 1939.

Mock, James R., and Larson, Cedric. *Words That Won the War.* Princeton, N.J.: Princeton University Press, 1939.

Mott, Frank Luther. *American Journalism: A History of Newspapers in the U.S. Through 250 Years, 1690–1940.* New York: Macmillan Co., 1941.

Naef, Weston. *The Collection of Alfred Stieglitz, Fifty Pioneers of Modern Photography.* New York: Viking Press, A Studio Book, and Metropolitan Museum of Art, 1978.

Newhall, Beaumont. *The History of Photography from 1839 to the Present.* New York: The Museum of Modern Art; Boston: Little, Brown & Company, 1982.

Ohrn, Karin B., and Hardt, Hanno. "Camera Reporters at Work, the Rise of the Photo Essay in Weimar Germany and the United States." Paper presented at the Eighth Biennial Convention of the American Studies Association, Memphis, Tennessee, 1981.

Page, Walter H. *A Publisher's Confession.* New York: Doubleday, Page & Company, 1923.

Palmer, Frederick. *With My Own Eyes.* Indianapolis: Bobbs-Merrill, 1933.

Photojournalism. New York: Time-Life Books, 1971.

Radest, Howard B. *Toward Common Ground: The Story of the Ethical Culture Societies in the United States.* New York: Frederick Ungar Publishing Co., 1969.

Rhode, Robert B., and McCall, Floyd W. *Press Photography, Reporting with a Camera.* New York: Macmillan Co., 1981.

Riis, Jacob. *How the Other Half Lives: Studies Among the Tenements of New York.* New York: Charles Scribner & Sons, 1890.

Rischin, Moses. *The Promised City.* Cambridge: Harvard University Press, 1962.

Rosenblum, Naomi. *A World History of Photography.* New York: Abbeville Press, 1984.

Rosenblum, Walter; Rosenblum, Naomi; and Trachtenberg, Alan. *America & Lewis Hine: Photographs 1904–1940.* Millerton, N.Y.: Aperture, 1977.

Rothstein, Arthur. *Photojournalism.* New York: American Photographic Book Publishing Co., 1956.

Salomon, Roger. *Twain and the Image of History.* New Haven: Yale University Press, 1961.

Schlesinger, Arthur. *Political and Social History of the United States.* New York: Macmillan Co., 1930.

――――. *The American as Reformer.* Cambridge: Harvard University Press, 1950.

Shaw, Renata, ed. *A Century of Photographs 1846–1946, Selected from the Collection of the Library of Congress.* Washington, D.C.: Library of Congress, 1980.

Tanner, Tony. *The Reign of Wonder.* London: Cambridge at the University Press, 1965.

Trachtenberg, Alan, ed. *Classic Essays on Photography.* New Haven, Conn.: Leete's Island Books, 1980.

Turner, Frederick Jackson. *The Frontier in American History.* New York: Henry Holt & Co., 1920.

Welling, William. *Photography in America.* New York: Thomas Crowell, 1978.

Whiting, John. *Photography Is a Language.* New York: Ziff-Davis, 1946.

Whitman, Walt. *Leaves of Grass Imprints.* Boston: Thayer & Eldridge, 1860.

――――. *New York Dissected.* New York: Rufus Rockwell Wilson, 1936.

――――. *Leaves of Grass.* Brooklyn, N.Y.: Privately printed, 1855. Facsimile reprint. New York: The Eakins Press, 1966.

――――. *Democratic Vistas, and Other Papers.* London. Walter Scott Publishing Co., 1888. Reprint. St. Clair Shores, Mich.: Scholarly Press, 1970.

Wood, James Playsted. *Magazines in the United States, Their Social and Economic Influence.* New York: The Ronald Press Company, 1949.

M A G A Z I N E S

Black, Alexander. "Photography in Fiction: 'Miss Jerry,' the First Picture Play." *Scribner's Magazine*, vol. 18, no. 3 (September 1895), pp. 348–60.

Blakenhorn, Heber. "The War of Morale." *Harper's Magazine*, vol. 139, no. 832 (September 1919), pp. 510–24.

Camera Work, nos. 1–50 (January 1903–June 1917). Edited by Alfred Stieglitz.

Clark, Sue Ainslie, and Wyatt, Edith. "Working-Girls' Budgets." *McClure's Magazine*, vol. 35, no. 6 (October 1910), pp. 595–614. Includes photographs by Hine.

Cockerill, John A. "Some Phases of Contemporary Journalism." *Cosmo*, vol. 13 (October 1892), pp. 695–701.

Folks, Homer. "Peace-Time Pioneers." *The World's Work*, vol. 38, no. 6, pp. 640–51. Includes photographs by Hine.

Hart, Russell. "The Outsiders." *Views: The Journal of Photography in New England*, vol. 8, no. 3 (Spring 1987), pp. 4–5, 22. Review of "Pictorialism: A Symposium on Art Photography."

Hendrick, Burton J. "Oxygenating a City." *McClure's Magazine*, vol. 35, no. 4 (August 1910), pp. 373–87. Includes photographs by Hine.

Hine, Lewis W. "The School Camera." *The Elementary School Teacher*, vol. 6 (March 1906), pp. 343–47. Includes photographs by Hine.

――――. "The School in the Park." *The Outlook*, vol. 83, no. 13 (July 28, 1906), pp. 712–19. Includes photographs by Hine and his students.

――――. "An Indian Summer." *The Outlook*, vol. 84, no. 9 (October 27, 1906), pp. 502–6. Includes photographs by Hine and his students.

――――. "The Silhouette in Photography." *The Photographic Times*, vol. 38, no. 11 (November 1906), pp. 488–90. Includes photographs by Hine and his students.

———. "Photography in the School." *The Photographic Times*, vol. 40, no. 8 (August 1908), pp. 227–32. Includes snapshots taken by Hine's students.

———. "The Question of the School Excursion." *Education*, vol. 29, no. 2 (October 1908), pp. 85–91. Not illustrated.

———. "Unto the Least of These." *Everybody's Magazine*, vol. 21, no. 1 (July 1909), pp. 75–87. Photographs and descriptions by Hine, acting on assignment for the National Child Labor Committee.

———. "Day Laborers Before Their Time, a Study in Pictures." *The Outlook*, vol. 93 (October 23, 1909), pp. 435–43. Photographs and descriptions by Hine, acting on assignment for the National Child Labor Committee.

The Illustrated American, vols. 1–2 (1890).

Jussim, Estelle, "Icons or Ideology: Stieglitz and Hine." *The Massachusetts Review*, vol. 19, no. 4 (Winter 1978), pp. 680–92.

Kellor, Ulrich F. "The Myth of Art Photography: A Sociological Analysis." *History of Photography*, vol. 8, no. 4 (December 1984), pp. 249–75.

Kellogg, Paul. "The Social Engineer in Pittsburgh." *The Outlook*, vol. 93 (September 24, 1909), pp. 153–69.

McCausland, Elizabeth. "Lewis W. Hine." *The Complete Photographer*, vol. 6, no. 31 (July 20, 1942), pp. 1979–83.

———. "Portrait of a Photographer." *Survey Graphic*, vol. 27, no. 10, pp. 502–5.

Newhall, Beaumont. "The Documentary Approach to Photography." *Parnassus*, vol. 10, no. 3 (March 1938), pp. 3–6.

The New York Times Mid-Week Pictorial, vol. 1, pt. 1–vol. 8, no. 12 (September 9, 1914–November 21, 1918).

Panzer, Mary. "Beauty and Utility: Rudolf Eikemeyer in the Gilded Age." *Views: The Journal of Photography in New England*, vol. 7, no. 3 (Spring 1986), pp. 8–11.

Pennell, Joseph. "Art and the Daily Newspaper." *The Nineteenth Century*, vol. 42 (October 1897), pp. 653–62.

Rayner, Paul. "Lewis W. Hine 1874–1940." *Ovo Magazine* (Winter 1977).

The Red Cross Magazine, vols. 14–16 (1919–20).

Road, Henry. "Big Brothers and Little." *Everybody's Magazine*, vol. 29, no. 2 (August 1913), pp. 246–56. Includes photographs by Hine.

Ross, Mary K. "New Faces for Old." *The Survey*, vol. 39, no. 26 (March 30, 1918), pp. 708–9.

Scott, Miriam. "At the Bottom." *Everybody's Magazine*, vol. 27 (October 1912), pp. 536–45. Includes photographs by Hine.

Sergeant, Elizabeth Shepley. "Toilers of the Tenements." *McClure's Magazine*, vol. 35, no. 3 (July 1910), pp. 231–38. Includes photographs by Hine.

Shorter, Clement K. "Illustrated Journalism: Its Past and Future." *Living Age*, vol. 221 (May 27, 1899), pp. 544–55.

Stange, Maren. "Gotham's Crime and Misery, Ideology and Entertainment in Jacob Riis's Lantern Slide Exhibitions." *Views: The Journal of Photography in New England*, vol. 8, no. 3 (Spring 1987), pp. 7–11.

Stein, Sally. "Making Connections with the Camera: Photography and Social Mobility in the Career of Jacob Riis." *Afterimage* (May 1983), pp. 9–16.

Trachtenberg, Alan. "Camera Work: Notes Toward an Investigation." *The Massachusetts Review*, vol. 19, no. 4 (Winter 1978), pp. 834–58.

LEWIS W. HINE BIBLIOGRAPHY

Scores of Hine's photographs and photo stories were reproduced in the progressive, popular, socialist, and trade press. For a comprehensive bibliography, see *America & Lewis Hine: Photographs 1904–1940* by Walter and Naomi Rosenblum and Alan Trachtenberg.

The citations that follow represent a selection of printed matter—leaflets, photo stories, Time Exposures—that I have either discussed or referred to in my text. An asterisk (*) next to a citation indicates materials that I have discovered.

National Child Labor Committee Printed Matter:

"Child Labor Stories for Children." *Child Labor Bulletin*. Vol. 2, no. 2. August 1913. Includes photographs by Hine.

"Fourteen Hours a Day in a Tenement Tailor Shop." Postcards by Hine. Appendixes B, C, and D, Child Labor Series No. 5, 1909.

*Hine, Lewis W. ("The Kodak," pseud.). "Night Scenes in the City of Brotherly Love." Leaflet No. 11. New York, May 1907.

*——— ("Small Kodak," pseud.). "The Burden Bearers." Leaflet No. 12. New York, 1907.

———. "The High Cost of Child Labor, a Birdseye View of This National Problem." Pamphlet No. 234. New York, June 1914.

———. "Can We Afford Child Labor?" *Child Labor Bulletin*. Vol. 3, no. 4. New York, February 1915.

Charities and the Commons/The Survey (pre-war photo stories):

"As They Come to Ellis Island." Vol. 20 (September 5, 1908), pp. 645–47.

"Children or Cotton?—Raising the Question of Cotton Picking in Texas." Vol. 31 (February 7, 1914), pp. 589–92.

"Construction Camps of the People." Vol. 23 (January 2, 1910), 448ff.

"Immigrant Types in the Steel District." Vol. 21 (January 2, 1909), pp. 581–89.

"Roving Children." Vol. 23 (January 1, 1910), 490ff.

*Untitled photo story about playgrounds. Vol. 15 (March 3, 1906), p. 829.

The Survey (Time Exposures):

"The Double Standard." Vol. 32 (April 4, 1914), p. 5.

"Girl Workers in a Cotton Mill." Vol. 31 (March 14, 1914), p. 737.

"In the Cool of the Evening." Vol. 32 (September 5, 1914), p. 556.

"School Opens at 6:00." Vol. 31 (February 21, 1914), p. 637.

"Three Bits of Testimony for Consumers of Shrimp and Oysters." Vol. 31 (February 28, 1914), p. 662.

Untitled. Vol. 32 (August 1, 1914), p. 446.

McCall's:

Dwight, Helen C. "Growing Up Like Father." Vol. 43, no. 1 (1915). Includes altered photographs by Hine.

Everybody's Magazine (World War I work):

"Playtime at the Training Camp—The Soldier's Life Is Not All Work." July 1918, pp. 66–67.

"The Stuff That Makes Our Fighting Force." September 1918, pp. 40–41.

"The Yankee Stew—A Bit Too Hot for the Kaiser." October 1918, pp. 52–53.

The Survey (work produced during the war and American Red Cross photographs):

"Few Are Their Belongings." Vol. 40 (August 10, 1918), cover.

"The Girls They Leave Behind Them." Vol. 32 (August 22, 1914), p. 217.

"The Merciful Invasion of St. Etienne." Vol. 41 (October 12, 1918), p. 38.

"War Time." Vol. 35 (January 29, 1916), cover.

The Survey (includes postwar photographs and Reconstruction photo stories):

"The Child's Burden in The Balkans." Vol. 42, cover, pp. 813–17.

"Let It Be That Peace Shall Rule." Vol. 43 (October 4, 1919), p. 19.

"The Pull of the Home Tie." Vol. 42 (July 31, 1919), p. 373.

"Refugees—In the Turkish Quarter." Vol. 42 (May 31, 1919), p. 373.

"They Departed into Their Own Country." Vol. 42 (August 2, 1919), pp. 661–65.

"The War and the Children." Vol. 43 (November 8, 1919), pp. 79–85.

The World's Work:

Folks, Homer. "Peace-Time Pioneers." Vol. 38 (October 1919), pp. 640–51. Includes photographs by Hine.

The Red Cross Magazine:

"Our All-American Army." Vol. 14 (February 1919), cover, pp. 41–45.

"The March of the Red Cross." Vol. 15 (April 1920), pp. 60–62.

A R C H I V E S

American Red Cross, National Headquarters, Photography Department, Washington, D.C.

Archives of American Art, Elizabeth McCausland Papers, New York, N.Y.

Butler Library, The Rare Book and Manuscript Library, Homer Folks Papers, Columbia University, New York, N.Y.

Commission on Archives and History, The United Methodist Church, Madison, N.J.

The Ethical Culture Schools, New York, N.Y.

International Museum of Photography at George Eastman House, Lewis W. Hine Collection, Rochester, N.Y.

Library of Congress, Manuscript Division, Papers of the National Child Labor Committee, Washington, D.C.

Library of Congress, Prints and Photographs Division, American Red Cross Collection, Washington, D.C.

National Child Labor Committee, New York, N.Y.

Social Welfare History Archives, Papers of Paul Kellogg and the Survey Associates, University of Minnesota, Minneapolis.

G A L L E R I E S

The Armstrong Gallery, New York, N.Y.

Alan Klotz, Photocollect, New York, N.Y.

Daniel Wolf Gallery, New York, N.Y.

A C K N O W L E D G M E N T S

"Maurice, five years old, four a refugee.
When he was a year old his father went to
war and the rest of his family became exiles."
(GEH)

A C K N O W L E D G M E N T S

In the seven years I spent researching the photographs and photo stories of Lewis Hine, I was fortunate to work with many exceptional people.

First, I would like to thank George Hobart, Curator of Photography, The Library of Congress, Prints and Photographs Division, Washington, D.C., for recognizing the importance of Hine's European work and for inviting me to curate and organize an exhibition. Also, I respectfully acknowledge Dr. Stephen Ostrow, Chief, and Dr. Renata Shaw, Assistant Chief, Prints and Photographs Division, for facilitating the show's existence.

My warmest thanks to Dr. Katherine Crum, Director of the Baruch Art Gallery, New York, for her energetic dedication in coordinating the show, "Lewis Hine in Europe: 1918–1919," and for arranging to have it travel to the Doris Freedman Gallery, Albright College, Reading, Pennsylvania, and the Art Gallery, State University of New York at Stony Brook, New York. I appreciate the efforts of the Institute for Research in History, New York, which cosponsored the exhibition.

During the period of my manuscript research, I was permitted to utilize Hine's photographs, negatives, and documentary materials at the International Museum of Photography at George Eastman House, Rochester, New York, at a time when access was restricted. Many thanks particularly to Andrew Eskind for providing me with a prototype of the Hine videodisc, Joanne Lukitsh for generously sharing her research on Hine, and Catherine Ritter for verifying data about the Hine archives.

Alan Trachtenberg, Maren Stange, and Jon Silverman read portions of the manuscript and offered invaluable criticism.

For service beyond the call of duty, kudos to David Klaassen, Archivist, Social Welfare History Archives, University of Minnesota, Minneapolis, Minnesota, and Elizabeth Hooks, Photography Department, American Red Cross, National Headquarters, Washington, D.C. I would also like to acknowledge Betty Thompson, Assistant Secretary, General Board of Global Ministries, Mission Education and Cultivation, The United Methodist Church, New York, for supporting my work from its inception as a research project. In addition, William Beal, Department of Archives, Commission on Archives and History, Madison, New Jersey, Alan Klotz of Photocollect, New York, Rita Silverstein of the Armstrong Gallery, New York, Judy Rich of the Ethical Culture School, New York, and the staffs of the Daniel Wolf Gallery, New York, and the National Child Labor Committee, New York, provided full access to their collections of early Hine photographs.

In 1984–85 I received fellowship support from the Ludwig Vogelstein Foundation, the New York State Council on the Arts, and the Rolf Kaltenborn Foundation. These grants enabled me to continue my research, curate the exhibition, and begin the writing.

I am enormously grateful to my editor, Walton Rawls, for his wit, wisdom, and historical knowledge of the first World War. My fond appreciation to Stephanie Bart-Horvath, whose insights into Hine's photographs are vividly reflected in the book's design.

Finally, for their wellspring of love and encouragement, I am grateful to those nearest and dearest—Irma Kaplan, Edward Kaplan, Meryl Belenko, Donna Henes, Amy Taubin, and Ursule Molinaro.

OTHERWISE UNCREDITED PHOTOGRAPHS